Salmon and Trout Farming in Norway

Salmon and Trout Farming in Norway

by

David J Edwards BSc PhD

Department of Animal Genetics and Breeding,
Agricultural University of Norway

Published by

 Fishing News Books Limited

Farnham, Surrey, England

First Published 1978

British Library CIP Data

Edwards, David John
   Salmon and trout farming in Norway
   1. Salmon   2. Trout   3. Fish-culture—Norway
   I. Title
   639'.375'5   SH 167.S 17

ISBN 0 85238 093 3

Front cover picture by Ola Sveen

Printed in Great Britain by Page Bros (Norwich) Ltd, Norwich

Contents

List of Figures

List of Tables

Publisher's Note

Dr. Edwards has worked with fish for over ten years, and published many articles and scientific papers on fish biology. In 1971 he was awarded a doctorate from the University College of North Wales, Marine Science Laboratories, Menai Bridge, for a thesis on the physiology of plaice. From 1971–1975 he was employed by the Fisheries Research Division, Ministry of Agriculture and Fisheries in New Zealand. Based at Rotorua, his job mainly concerned the culture of grass carp as a biological control for aquatic weeds. Late in 1975 Dr. Edwards joined the Department of Animal Genetics and Breeding, Agricultural University of Norway, to work on aspects of salmon and trout culture, notably selective breeding.

Acknowledgements

The author wishes to thank all the fish farmers and scientists who provided information or photographs for use in this book. Special thanks go to the following: Professor Harald Skjervold, Department of Animal Genetics and Breeding, Agricultural University of Norway; Mr Lars Bull-Berg, Norwegian Fish Farmers' Association, Oslo; Mr Thor Mowinckel, A/S Mowi, Bergen; Mr Olav Egeland, Øksna Bruk A/S, Sandnes; Mr Erling Osland, Eros-Laks A/S, Bjordal; Mr Oscar Torrissen, Torris-Laks A/S, Halsa; Mr Ragnar Sjåvik, Herøy Lakseoppdrett A/S; Messrs T Skretting and Finn Hallingstad, T Skretting A/S, Stavanger; Ms Reidun Haugen, Norsk Landbrukskjemi A/S (Norwegian agent for Astra-Ewos A/B), Lørenskog; Erland Austreng, Department of Poultry and Fur-Animal Science, Agricultural University of Norway; Messrs Vidar Vassvik, Terje Refstie and Knut Gunnes, Fish Breeding Experimental Station, Sunndalsøra; and Dr Tore Håstein, Norwegian Veterinary Institute, Oslo.

I am indebted to my wife, Sheila, for editing the manuscript, Mrs Grethe Tuven for drawing diagrams, and Mrs Reidun Pettersen and Miss Anne Karin Sollund for typing the final manuscript.

Above all my thanks go to Dr Trygve Gjedrem, Department of Animal Genetics and Breeding, Agricultural University of Norway, and Mr Arne Kittelsen, Fish Breeding Experimental Station, Sunndalsøra. They provided a wealth of information and corrected and improved the first draft of the manuscript.

1 Development of Salmonid Farming in Norway

INDUSTRIAL FISH

Norway is one of the world's leading fishing nations. In the early seventies the total annual catch of wet fish by Norwegian vessels varied between about 2.4 and 2.8 million tonnes. However, only 25–28% of this was used for direct human consumption. The rest was 'industrial' fish, mostly for reduction to fish meal and oil.

Industrial fish is an essential component of many animal foods, and in the past it formed a high proportion of the total ration. For most domestic animals the fish meal content of modern foods is small, for example in pig diets about 2% by weight (though considerably more by cost), and the diet is artificially supplemented with essential amino acids previously only widely available in fish meal.

The commercial farming of fish for human food has been practised for centuries in some parts of the world, especially in Asia, mainly using fish species which are either herbivorous or omnivorous and farmed in semi-natural pond conditions where most of the fishes' dietary requirements for animal protein are met from natural production in the pond. Fish farming began in western Europe and North America relatively recently, and in these areas has concentrated on the production of high-value, carnivorous species. These species are usually cultured intensively, *ie* in more or less closely controlled conditions and densely crowded. In such conditions the fish farmer has to supply almost all the fishes' food, and in the case of salmon and trout this must contain a high proportion of animal protein. Most of this usually comes from industrial fish, which is fed to the salmon and trout either directly or after conversion into fish meal for inclusion in pelleted diets. Many studies have been made to try to find substitutes for fish meal in salmonid diets, but so far these have shown inferior salmonid growth when the fish content of the food was reduced below about

1

20%, and current practical diets contain considerably more than this (Chapter 8).

Norway, therefore, unlike many other European countries, has a supply of suitable basic foodstuffs potentially capable of supporting an enormous salmon and trout farming industry.

DANISH-STYLE TROUT CULTURE

With the availability of large quantities of suitable food from the commercial capture fishery, and the equally important supply of skilled labour in this industry, it was natural that Norway should take interest in the rapid expansion of fresh water rainbow trout farming which occurred in neighbouring Denmark. Trout farming started in Denmark in about 1890 and, apart from a short boom just before the First World War, developed slowly until 1950 when annual production was about 2,000 tonnes. Since then production has increased rapidly, reaching a peak of 16,770 tonnes in 1975. It now seems likely to stabilize at around 15,000 tonnes per annum, the limitations on future expansion being the shortage of new suitable sites and pollution problems caused by faeces and waste food from existing farms.

Unfortunately Norway is climatically not a very suitable country for this type of trout farming, in which rainbow trout are grown to 'portion' size of 150–250 g in fresh water ponds. The main problem is one of low water temperatures. Growth of trout is closely dependent on water temperature, and below about 4 or 5°C little growth can be expected. Even in the south of Norway most fresh waters have temperatures well below 4°C, and often approaching 0°C, for almost half the year, resulting in a short growing season for trout. Though a number of Danish-style trout farms did start operations in Norway, they found it impossible to grow portion-size fish at prices competitive with foreign producers. Those which did not close down, therefore, have changed over to producing either larger food fish (Chapter 2) or fingerlings big enough to tolerate the transition to life in sea water (Chapter 4).

CULTURE IN SEA WATER

Temperature

The sea round most of Norway's coast does not have this disadvantage of low winter temperature. The warm waters of the Gulf Stream approach the Norwegian coast from the south west and flow up the long west coast until meeting the cold water of the Arctic. Another current, which is cold in winter, flows out of the Baltic sea and up the west coast of Norway as a coastal stream. The Baltic and Gulf Stream waters tend to mix progressively as they flow north together (*Fig 1*). The influence of the Gulf Stream prevents the sea water off the Norwegian coast from freezing during winter, though enclosed areas of water inside the fjords do freeze over.

Maximum and minimum annual temperatures of sea water at a number of places along the Norwegian coast are shown in *Fig 2*. Temperatures shown are means of routine recordings at 4 m depth taken by ships over many years. Apart from the small east coast, which is entirely under the influence of the Baltic current, the sea water off the coast of Norway up to about 68° of latitude has a normal annual minimum temperature above 4°C, and for much of this area the minimum is above 5°C. In these areas, therefore, growth of salmonid fishes held in the sea can be expected to continue all year round, though of course it will be much faster in summer than in winter.

Salmonids require a high level of dissolved oxygen in the water, and therefore do not tolerate a high temperature. Temperatures above 18–20°C are considered undesirable, but summer sea water temperatures off the Norwegian coast only approach this in the extreme south and east. The areas of Norway's coast in which water temperatures are most suitable for the culture of salmonids are shown in *Fig 2*.

Shelter

If one looks at a map of the Norwegian coastline one is immediately impressed by its broken-up and indented nature. In addition to the famous fjords there are many islands of all sizes. These irregularities provide many areas of water sheltered from the worst effects of wave and wind action. Such sheltered areas can be good sites for salmon and trout farms, which could otherwise be vulnerable to damage by storm.

Development of sea culture

The natural suitability of Norway's coast for salmonid production led to a change from conventional fresh water production of rainbow trout to sea water production. This subsequently made the culture of salmon possible.

The first recorded attempt to grow rainbow trout in sea water in Norway was in 1912, but little progress was made until the fifties, when pioneers like the Vik brothers at Sykkylven carried out trials which

3

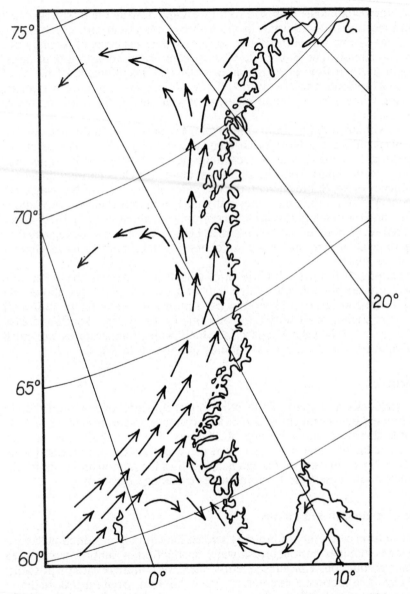

Fig 1. Sea water currents off the Norwegian coast. The Gulf Stream provides
temperatures suitable for salmonid culture on the west coast. (*From Skjervold, 1975*).

4

Place	Sea temperature			No. months over						
	Mean	Min.	Max.	4°	5°	6°	7°	8°	9°	10°
Varangerfjord	5.5	2.0	10.2	7	6	5	3	3	2	1
Vardø	5.3	2.6	8.7	7	6	4	4	2	0	0
Nordkyn	5.6	2.9	8.9	8	7	5	4	3	0	0
Revsbotn	5.9	3.2	8.9	9	7	5	4	3	0	0
Lopphavet	6.2	2.9	10.4	9	7	6	5	3	3	2
Malangen	6.2	2.8	10.3	8	7	6	5	3	3	2
Vågsfjorden	6.9	2.9	12.0	9	8	6	5	5	3	3
Andfjorden	7.0	3.2	12.0	9	8	6	6	5	3	3
Vestfjorden	7.4	3.2	12.9	9	8	7	6	5	4	3
Hestmanøy	7.5	3.8	12.6	10	8	7	6	5	5	3
Ylvingen	7.8	4.3	12.7	12	8	8	6	5	5	3
Folla	8.6	4.7	13.6	12	10	8	7	6	5	5
Kjeungskjær	8.3	4.9	12.8	12	11	8	7	5	5	5
Smøla	8.7	5.1	13.5	12	12	8	8	6	5	5
Hustadvika	8.6	4.6	13.7	12	10	8	7	6	5	4
Breisundet	9.0	4.5	14.3	12	10	8	8	6	5	5
Stad	8.8	4.6	13.9	12	10	8	8	6	6	5
Sognesjøen	9.1	4.5	14.6	12	10	8	8	6	6	5
Korsfjorden	9.4	4.2	15.4	12	10	8	8	7	6	5
Sletta	9.1	4.3	14.7	12	10	8	8	7	6	5
Jæren	9.0	3.6	15.3	10	9	8	8	7	6	5
Lindenes	9.0	2.9	16.1	10	8	8	7	7	6	5
Torungen	9.0	1.9	17.1	8	8	7	7	7	6	5
Ferder	9.0	1.1	17.6	9	7	7	7	6	6	5

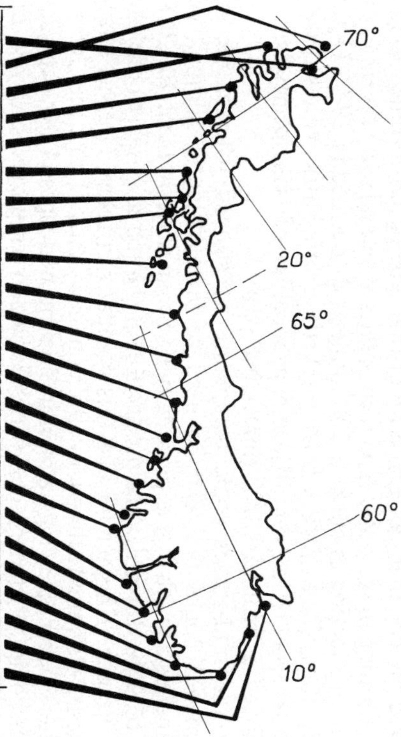

Fig 2. Sea water temperatures on Norway's west coast. The areas within the dotted line are the most suitable for salmonid culture. *(From Skjervold, 1975).*

5

B

showed the commercial feasibility of this type of fish farming. Rainbow trout farming in sea water expanded in the sixties and early seventies, until a peak production of about 2,200 tonnes was reached in 1974. Unfortunately there have always been marketing difficulties with Norwegian rainbow trout (Chapter 10), and production of this species has now stabilized at around 1,800 tonnes per year.

In the mid-sixties some companies questioned whether the same techniques could not also be used to farm Atlantic salmon, which commands a much higher price at market than rainbow trout. In 1965 the firm of A/S Mowi planned production of salmon in large sea enclosures near Bergen (Chapter 6), and this company is today Norway's largest producer of farmed salmon. In 1969, on the island of Hitra, the Grøntvedt brothers began growing salmon in floating net cages. Their cage design has become a standard one which is widely employed today in many farms (Chapter 7).

The greatest constraints on the development of salmon farming were the unreliable supply and erratic price of smolts and, to a lesser extent, the availability of equipment. The construction of several large private and government units to produce salmon smolts for sale to fish farmers for growing-on in sea water paved the way for a phenomenal rise in the number of salmon farms during the early seventies. Manufacturers of fish farming equipment, foodstuffs and chemicals have helped this expansion, and it is now possible to buy, ready-made, everything necessary to start and run a fish farm.

In 1976, production of salmon passed that of rainbow trout, reaching almost 2,000 tonnes, and the expansion in output is continuing (Chapter 12). In 1977 there were probably around 400 salmon or trout farms in Norway producing food fish, but many of these are very small and some only work intermittently. About 200 farms have a regular annual production of 1 tonne or more. Production figures given in this book are based on amounts declared by farmers to the Norwegian Fish Farmers' Association. Since most farms are small, however, it is highly probable that many farmers are able to find local outlets for part of their production which they neglect to record. The true total annual production is, therefore, certainly higher than stated here.

Social considerations

Norway, in common with many countries today, faces problems with a drift of human population away from rural areas into towns and cities. This results in social difficulties for both the donor and recipient areas as well as much individual unhappiness. In Norway depopulation is especially bad in the isolated valley and island communities of which there are so many all the way up the west coast. The main industries in these areas are farming and fishing. The fishing is often only seasonal, and many of the farms are very small, consisting of only two or three hectares of land on which the soil is often poor. The income obtainable from such small-scale farming is frequently insufficient to provide a family with all the modern aids to a comfortable life, with the result that many, especially the young, leave to seek their fortunes elsewhere.

It is precisely some of the areas worst affected by depopulation which are most suitable for salmon and trout farming in sea water. With modern methods of cage culture (Chapter 7) new fish farms can start small and grow gradually. It is consequently not beyond the economic means of country people to get started in this business, and the high-value crop of fish produced can enable people to stay in their traditional homes by supplementing their income from conventional sources. The government has recognised the potential social benefits, and encourages the development of salmonid farming in depopulated areas by guaranteeing loans through the Regional Development Fund and the Agricultural Development Fund.

It would have been possible for salmonid farming in the future to develop in one of two ways. Either production could have become concentrated in a few large units, or spread into a larger number of smaller units. To ensure that the benefits of this new industry are spread as much as possible, a law was passed in 1973 limiting the size of new sea farms to a production capacity of $8,000 \text{ m}^3$. In the usual type of farm, using floating net cages, this would impose a limit of $16 \times 500 \text{ m}^3$ or $26 \times 300 \text{ m}^3$ cages, capable of producing comfortably about 60 tonnes of salmon annually. Farms which were already larger than this in 1973, however, are exempt from the size restriction.

7

2 The Production Cycle

NATURAL LIFE CYCLES

Species

Only those species of the salmon family of interest to fish culturists will be considered here. These species can be broadly divided into two groups on the basis of their life cycles, *ie* (1) species which spend their whole lives in fresh water, and (2) anadromous species, which reproduce and spend the juvenile part of their lives in fresh water, but then migrate to the sea, where most of their growth occurs.

Of those salmonid species found in Norway, Atlantic salmon (*Salmo salar*), sea trout (*Salmo trutta*) and pink salmon (*Oncorhynchus gorbuscha*) are anadromous. Pink salmon are a Pacific species which has recently appeared in some Norwegian fjords and seems to be spreading its range progressively southwards. This species arrived in Norway as a result of Russian experiments involving the transplantation of many millions of fertilized eggs from the Pacific coast of the Soviet Union to the rivers of the Kola peninsula and the White Sea. The brown trout, classified as the same species as sea trout, and brook trout (*Salvelinus fontinalis*), a species of char originally introduced from North America, are usually wholly fresh water species. Some races of Arctic char (*Salvelinus alpinus*) spend the whole of their lives in fresh water, usually in fairly deep lakes, but other races form sea-run populations. Rainbow trout (*Salmo gairdnerii*), another species introduced from North America, in Norway are of a strain which naturally spends all its life in fresh water. They will not spawn naturally in Norway's cold fresh waters, so all populations must be artificially maintained by repeatedly stocking waters with hatchery-reared juveniles. Once above about 35 grams in weight, however, rainbow trout can be acclimatized to life in sea water.

8

Spawning

All these species naturally spawn in fresh water. Except for non-migratory Arctic char, which lay their eggs in lakes, spawning typically occurs in the head-waters and tributary streams of rivers, though it can occur anywhere in a river if the substrate is suitable. In spawning streams the water is shallow, cold and clean, and the stream bed on which the eggs are deposited is of clean stones and gravel free of fine silt which might overlay and smother the eggs. Usually the female fish will excavate a depression, called a redd, in the gravel with her tail, and deposit her eggs into this. The male fish then discharges his sperm over the eggs to effect fertilization. The fertilized eggs are covered with gravel to a depth of several centimetres.

Since most salmonid species spawn in these head waters the adults must undergo a 'spawning migration' upstream before spawning, regardless of whether their previous home was a river, lake or the sea. Spawning normally occurs in autumn, but some species may begin to move up-river months before this. Salmon can enter the rivers at any time of the year except late winter. The spawning migration in mature trout is triggered by environmental conditions associated with an increase in water flow in the stream.

Pacific salmon normally die after spawning. Mortality is fairly high also in Atlantic salmon, especially in males, but some spent fish (or kelts) survive to return to the sea. Such fish may return to the river to spawn again, but normally not until two years later. Survival of trout and char after spawning is usually good, and many individuals return to spawn again in subsequent years.

Development

Development of eggs in Norwegian fresh waters is very slow over the winter due to the low water temperature. The time eggs take to develop at a given temperature is different for different species, and this will be considered in more detail later as it relates to hatchery practice (Chapter 4). However, generally speaking, eggs spawned in October-November will not become eyed (*ie* the eyes of the embryo can be seen as two black dots) until the following February, and eggs hatch in April or May. The newly hatched fry, or alevins, live for the first few weeks of life on their yolk sacs, the remains of the food supplies from the egg. When most of the yolk sac has been used up, the fry become active and leave the protection of the redds to begin searching for food. This is referred to as 'swim-up', and fry often reach this stage of development around June.

During their first and second summers the young fish feed and grow, at the same time tending to move downstream from the spawning areas to richer feeding grounds. Some species develop vertical stripes on the sides of their bodies and are referred to as 'parr'.

From this stage onwards no basic change occurs in the life-style of those salmonid species which spend their whole lives in fresh water. They simply feed and grow until they themselves are ready to mature and spawn. The time taken to reach sexual maturity differs between species, races, areas of the country (climate) and environmental factors such as food abundance.

Migration to and from the sea

Amongst the species which migrate to sea some, *ie* Atlantic salmon and sea trout, undergo a clear physiological pre-adaptation to life in sea water while still in fresh water by smolting. In addition to internal changes in the salt-regulating mechanisms of the body, the appearance and behaviour of the fish changes. Most noticeably, a sub-cutaneous layer of guanin is laid down, concealing the parr markings and giving the sides of the fish a silvery colour. The tail of salmon often develops a black edge, and the fish change from swimming against the current to moving with it. Migratory char, though they undergo some physiological adaptation prior to seaward migration, do not go through the same clear change of body proportion and colour as Atlantic salmon and sea trout, and therefore perhaps cannot be said to truly smolt. Pink salmon can migrate to sea at a very early stage of development, virtually as fry. Downstream migration of young fish to the sea in spring is thought to be triggered by high water flows and rising temperatures.

After anything from one to five year's growth in the sea, the fish are ready to return to the rivers to spawn. All migratory salmonids show a remarkable 'homing instinct', by which a very large proportion of them are able to find the river in which they were themselves spawned. Many people believe that the fish are able to detect 'pheromones', *ie* chemical substances released by other fish in the river and present in very low concentration in the water.

ARTIFICIAL CULTURE

When salmonids are cultured artificially in hatcheries or fish farms the stages in production must broadly follow the natural life cycle. However, by manipulating the fishes' environment some modifications can be made to suit the convenience of the culturist. Also, the proportion of the fishes' life cycle which is artificially controlled varies according to the purpose for which the fish are being cultured.

Fish for angling and commercial capture

The species most often cultured for release to supplement natural populations of fish for angling or commercial capture are Atlantic salmon, sea trout, brown trout and rainbow trout. Some brook trout and Arctic char are also produced, but in Norwegian lakes overpopulation with the latter species is a more frequent problem than poor recruitment.

Fish reared for re-stocking purposes are of course grown in captivity for only the early part of their lives, then released to grow in the wild. Frequently release is at the smolt stage of development in the case of those species which undergo this physiological change, and as fingerlings of 10–100 g for other species. In a few cases larger fish are released, but put-and-take fishing is not common in Norway. Many millions of salmon and brown trout fry are liberated.

Norway has thousands of lakes and streams, most of which support salmonids, and a tradition of fishing. Angling is a popular pastime for Norwegians, and a valuable asset to the tourist industry. In summer, angling is carried out using rod and line methods and a variety of flies, lures and baits. Static fresh waters are frozen over during winter, but angling continues 'eskimo-style' using handlines through holes bored in the ice with a special instrument resembling a giant corkscrew. Traditionally, Norwegians ice-fish lying prone with only a reindeer skin or other thin insulation between them and the ice, and this technique is still common today especially in the northern regions of Troms and Finnmark. Where access to lakes by road is possible, however, the modern Norwegian is just as likely to drive his car onto the ice and fish from the comfort of a heated cab. Though brown trout are caught under the ice, the salmonid fish most commonly captured by this method is the Arctic char, which remains more active at winter water temperatures.

Commercial netting for salmonids is carried out both in the sea and in inland lakes. Especially in inland areas, many of the fishermen only fish part-time to supplement their incomes from small-scale farming. Several varieties of traps and gill-nets are used.

Most of Norway is relatively free of heavy industrial pollution but, as in other developed countries, human use of waterways is sometimes harmful to fish populations. All Norway's electric power is at present generated by hydro-electric power stations. As already mentioned, most salmonid species undergo an upstream migration prior to spawning, and the erection of dams, which are an intrinsic part of hydro-electric

11

schemes, puts an insurmountable barrier between the fish and their breeding grounds. Usually a 'fish ladder' or 'fish pass' is built alongside the dam to allow migratory fish to get upstream past the obstruction, but even so fewer fish are likely to reach the spawning grounds than before the power scheme was built. The young produced by those individuals which do succeed in spawning are also subject to mortality as they pass through the turbines of the power station on their way downstream. Where dams do not have fish passes the natural population of migratory fish in the river is completely destroyed in a few years. Another hazard is the rapid water flows in the tailraces of hydro-electric power stations. These can attract migratory fish away from their proper spawning river even when there is no obstruction on the river itself. Whilst some of these fish doubtless eventually find their way back into the river, many others probably exhaust themselves trying to ascend the flow from the turbines and fail to reach the spawning grounds.

The State Electricity Board is fully aware of these problems and their public relations implications, and is bound by law to release young fish to make up for the damage done by power schemes. Other hatcheries are owned by associations formed by the owners of fishing rights in a particular area, and by local and national government. Altogether there are about 150 hatcheries in Norway producing salmonids for release into natural waters. Their operation resembles, though is perhaps less efficient than, that of units producing small fish for subsequent on-growing to market size in captivity (Chapters 3 and 4).

Fish for food

In Norway, Atlantic salmon and rainbow trout cultured for the table market are kept for the whole of their life cycles in captivity. The production cycle of each is divided into two parts.

The first stage of production deals with the cultivation of fish from the egg through the early stages of life, predominantly in fresh water. The end products of this phase of production are salmon smolts, and rainbow trout of 50–150 g. The latter are referred to in this book as 'fingerlings'.

Methods for producing smolts and fingerlings are similar whether the fish are intended for release to supplement natural populations or to be kept in captivity for their whole lives. However, in the latter case production tends to be concentrated in a few large and fairly new units (*Fig* 3), whereas there are many small units, some of them quite old, producing young fish for release into natural waters. The producers of future food fish, therefore, tend to have more modern equipment and use more advanced techniques.

Fig 3. A large, modern smolt and fingerling unit at Sunndalsøra, run by the Department of Animal Genetics and Breeding, Agricultural University of Norway. (*Photograph: Ola Sveen*).

The second phase in food fish production is the growing-on of fish to harvest size. In the early days some farms produced portion-size trout like those popular in the rest of Europe. Nowadays all salmon and trout in Norway are grown to as large a size as possible before harvest (*Fig* 4).

Production in fresh water ponds. In spite of the unfavourably low water temperatures prevalent in Norway, a few fresh water trout farms do still successfully produce rainbow trout for the table market using earth ponds of the Danish type (*Fig* 5).

These farms are confined to the low-lying areas of the extreme south and east of the country. They obtain their water supplies either from springs or from lowland rivers which do not have their origins in the mountains and whose temperatures are therefore higher than 'typical' Norwegian rivers. Even in the most favourable sites, however, water temperatures still fall too low for trout growth to continue during the coldest three months of the year, December-February, and in most areas for longer than this. Frequently ponds freeze solid in winter. Consequently most farms operate only in the warmer half or two-thirds of the year and do not carry any fish over the winter. They buy rainbow trout

13

Fig 4. Rainbow trout grown in the sea to a mean weight of 2–3 kg.

Fig 5. Earth ponds for fresh water production of rainbow trout.

14

fingerlings of 50–100 g in spring from specialist producers, and slaughter all their stock in autumn of the same year. Fish growth during summer can be surprisingly good, probably because of the very long day length, and an average weight of around 750 g at slaughter is frequently obtained. Much of the fish grown in this way is used to produce 'rakefisk', a rather strong-smelling Norwegian delicacy made by fermenting trout at low temperature for several months. Fish prepared in this way commands a very high price.

Very few fresh water farms in Norway overwinter their fish in ponds. By far the largest of those which does so is that of the company Øksna Bruk A/S at Sandnes near Stavanger (*Fig* 6). This company produces up to 100 metric tons of rainbow trout for the table market annually, but its output of food fish is declining in favour of the increased production of fingerlings for sale for on-growing in the sea (see below).

The Øksna Bruk farm was established in 1961 to the design of Danish specialists. It is therefore modelled closely on the Danish system of earth ponds. Ponds are arranged in two rows with a central canal carrying incoming water from a dam across the Figgjo river upstream of the farm. Flow from the canal into the ponds is by gravity and the ingoing water to each pond passes through a screened inlet. At the other end of each pond

Fig 6. Øksna Bruk A/S, at Sandnes near Stavanger, is Norway's largest fresh water rainbow trout farm.
(*Photograph: T Skretting A/S, Øksna Bruk A/S*).

15

is a similar screened outlet through which water falls into subsidiary ponds and outflow canals, which are also stocked with fish. Before discharge into the river, outflow water passes through a 2,000m³ sedimentation pond to remove suspended matter. Øksna Bruk has about 20 production ponds, ranging in size from 0.05 to 1 ha and of 1–2.5m depth. In summer a 1,000m³/h electric pump re-circulates water from the lowest production pond on the farm to the intake canal. In addition, a compressor is used to blow air through perforated plastic pipes at the bottom of each pond to ensure that the water remains well oxygenated.

Trout stocked into the growing ponds in the autumn of their first year are harvested in autumn one year later at a mean weight of around 1kg. To harvest fish from the earth ponds a seine net is used to confine the fish to a small area (*Fig 7*). They are then removed either by hand using nets or, more usually, by a vacuum fish pump.

Sea water production. In the vast majority of rainbow trout farms and all salmon farms, however, the smolts or fingerlings are transferred to sea water for growing-on to harvest size. Except where otherwise stated, the rest of this book deals with the production of salmon and rainbow trout in the usual Norwegian way, *ie* cultivation of fingerlings or smolts in fresh water followed by on-growing to slaughter or maturity in the sea.

Fig 7. Harvesting rainbow trout from earth ponds. (*Photograph: T Skretting A/S*).

16

SEQUENCE OF PRODUCTION

Two basic principles must be appreciated before the production cycles for salmon and rainbow trout can be understood.

(1) Growth rates of both species are slower in fresh water than in sea water. This applies especially to salmon which, under natural conditions in Norway, may require over four year's growth in fresh water to reach the smolt stage of development, at which they weigh only about 30 g. After migrating to the sea, however, the same fish may reach a weight of 6–8 kg during their next two years. If kept in fresh water after smoltification mortality is high and growth is very slow.

This growth difference is less extreme in rainbow trout and, as they do not spawn naturally in Norway or have to migrate to the sea, it is difficult to compare their natural growth in fresh and salt water. However, in fish farms rainbow trout may reach a mean weight of 70 g, at which size they can tolerate transfer to the sea, by the spring following that in which they were hatched. If grown-on in sea water they may average up to 3 kg by the autumn of the next year, whereas if kept in fresh water half this weight would be more likely.

The main reason for faster growth of rainbow trout in the sea than in fresh water in Norway is assumed to be the higher winter temperature of the former. For salmon the additional and even more important factor that is involved is that this species undergoes a physiological pre-adaptation to sea water by smolting. If kept in fresh water after this stage of development the fish are not physiologically suited to their environment and cannot be expected to grow well.

The costs of maintaining hatchery facilities, of overheads and labour, all tend to be proportionate to time, whereas return is proportionate to fish growth. The culturist therefore wants his fish to grow as fast as possible, and one of the most important modifications he makes to the natural life cycles of his fish is to reduce the slow-growing fresh water stage of their development to as short a time as possible.

Because of their naturally long fresh water life this is especially important for salmon. By optimal feeding, all Norwegian units are able to reduce the time taken for salmon to reach the smolt stage of development to a little over two years. By heating the water supply to egg trays and fry tanks most units routinely produce a high proportion of one-year-old smolts, ie fish which smolt in the spring of their second year.

(2) The price per kilo at market is greater for larger fish (see Chapter 10). The farmer therefore wants to grow his fish to as big a size as possible.

In practice, the maximum size attainable is determined by the age at which the fish become sexually mature. As salmon mature, their growth

17

rate of 'meat' slows down because most of the food they eat is used for development of their gonads. Furthermore, the quality of their flesh also deteriorates, and the mortality rate increases. It is necessary, therefore, that salmon to be sold for food should be harvested before the onset of sexual maturity. Normally, salmon stocked into the sea as smolts in the spring of one year will mature in the autumn two years later. Accordingly they must be harvested at the latest in summer two years after entering the sea. In fact they are normally harvested a little earlier than this, in spring, partly because their cages are needed for the new crop of smolts and partly to get them to market before the fishing season for wild salmon starts. Only brood stock are kept in the sea for longer. For rainbow trout, harvesting before maturity is even more vital. Mortality of trout confined to sea water when they become fully mature is very high, especially for males, and 50% or more of the stock can be lost. Rainbow trout normally mature during their second winter in the sea, and are therefore harvested in autumn before this.

The sequence of production for salmon and rainbow trout through fresh and sea water phases is shown in *Fig* 8.

Because the costs of buildings and equipment are high, smolt and fingerling production in fresh water is mostly concentrated into few, large farms. Some of these belong to big companies which also grow-on fish in the sea, but others sell their young fish to the many smaller fish farming companies which specialize in rearing them through to harvest. Some companies use fixed fish enclosures to grow-on salmonids in sea water (Chapter 6) but the majority use floating net cages (Chapter 7). This latter production method is very flexible as regards size and cost, and can be started with relatively little capital. Consequently there are many small farms producing fish in this way.

Rainbow trout

When kept in water at ambient temperature, mature rainbow trout can be stripped artificially as soon as the temperature begins to rise in spring, *ie* in March-May according to latitude. Even with optimal feeding, young fish resulting from such spawnings will not grow large enough to tolerate transfer to sea water (over about 50 g) until the next spring. After transfer to the sea they are grown for $1\frac{1}{2}$ years until the following autumn, when they are harvested as $2\frac{1}{2}$-year-old fish. Farmers frequently then have empty cages until the following spring when the next stock of fingerlings is ready. This is the traditional cycle of production of rainbow trout in Norway.

Recently a shorter production cycle has been gaining popularity, led by the enterprise of the company Øksna Bruk A/S. By holding brood fish in

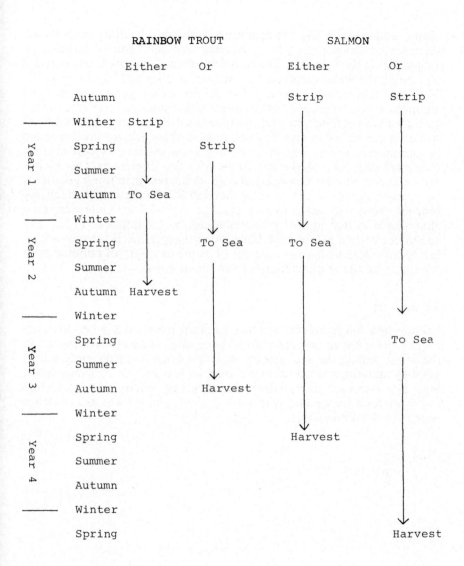

Fig 8. Cycles of production for salmon and rainbow trout in Norway.

spring water, which has a temperature of about 7°C all through winter, their sexual development is accelerated and they can be stripped in January or early February. Development of eggs and fry is also speeded by heating the water supplying the incubating trays and fry unit to 10°C. This gets the growth of young fish off to such a good start that the company is able to produce fish large enough to tolerate transfer to the sea by the autumn of their first year. As rainbow trout can only be left for one winter in the sea, otherwise they will mature, these fish must be harvested in autumn exactly one year after stocking in the sea, *ie* as 1½-year-old fish. Cages are then re-stocked immediately with new fingerlings. Though fish grown in this way are obviously smaller at harvest than those grown for 1½ years in the sea, the cycle of production for the sea unit is effectively reduced from two years to one and the period with empty cages is eliminated, so that annual production can be considerably higher and capital turnover is accelerated. Other fingerling producers are now adopting Øksna Bruk's methods, and in 1976 the tonnages of rainbow trout produced by the two techniques were about equal.

Salmon

Salmon take longer to produce than rainbow trout, mainly because they require either one or two years to reach the smolt stage of development. In their first year in the sea, growth rates of salmon are frequently not as good as rainbow trout; a salmon ending its first marine year may weigh only 1 kg. However, because they take longer to mature, salmon can stay in the sea for a full second year, during which time growth to an average weight of 4–5 kg is usual.

3 Fresh Water Supplies and Hatchery Siting

The most important factor determining the suitability of a potential site for a hatchery or other fresh water salmonid unit is the quantity and quality of the available water supply. Chemical and physical characteristics of the water must be tested regularly for at least one year, and preferably longer, before investment in building is considered. In Norway, time and expense on investigating unsuitable waters can frequently be saved by consulting the records of the local *Landbruksselskaper*, the county authorities concerned with land and water use, and the regional office of the Directorate of Wildlife and Freshwater Fisheries.

TEMPERATURE

Water temperature is the most important limitation on the suitability of fresh water supplies for salmonid units in Norway. Egg hatching and fish growth rates closely depend on water temperature. Temperatures of around 15–18°C are considered optimal for the growth of rainbow trout, and for most other salmonids slightly lower temperatures are preferable. The upper lethal limit is around 24–27°C, but at temperatures above about 20°C appetite and growth are reduced and the fish become more sensitive to water-borne pollutants and to attack by disease organisms.

In practice Norwegian fresh water temperatures are usually too low, rather than too high, for salmonid culture. The lower lethal limit is around −0.5°C but little growth can be expected below 5°C. The temperature of most surface fresh waters in Norway approaches 0°C for several months of the year.

Electrical heating

To obtain better fish growth and to manipulate the time when eggs hatch

21

c

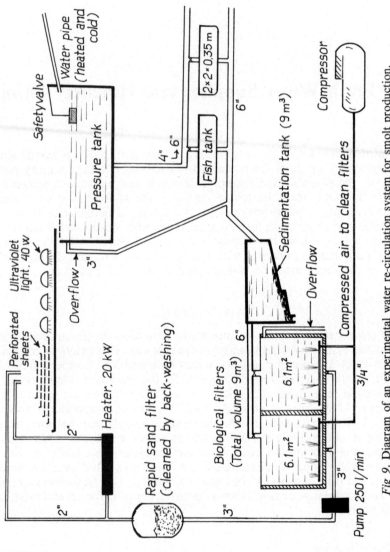

Fig 9. Diagram of an experimental water re-circulation system for smolt production. (From Risa and Skjervold, 1975).

Safetyvalve

Water pipe (heated and cold)

Pressure tank

Ultraviolet light. 40 w

Perforated sheets

Heater. 20 kW

Overflow

Rapid sand filter (cleaned by back-washing)

Fish tank

2 × 2 × 0.35 m

Sedimentation tank (9 m³)

Biological filters (Total volume 9 m³)

6.1 m²

6.1 m²

Overflow

Compressed air to clean filters

Compressor

Pump 250 l/min

6"

6"

4"

3"

2"

2"

3"

3"

6"

3/4"

many hatcheries have installed equipment to provide heated fresh water. For most, electric heating is used. This is so expensive that it is normally only used to warm the relatively small quantities of water needed to supply the egg hatching trays and early fry tanks. The larger amount of water supplying the fish growing tanks is heated electrically in a few units producing trout for re-stocking natural waters. But this is only done where the hatchery is run by the Electricity Board near a hydro-electric power station, from which free electricity is available. It is doubtful whether it could ever be justified economically by the value of the fish produced.

Re-circulation

Systems for re-circulating electrically heated water are being developed, since it is estimated that these could reduce the cost of power by about 75%. So far, only fairly simple re-circulation systems are used commercially for egg hatching and smolt production. A more elaborate experimental prototype system which has been used to speed the growth of young salmon at the Fish Breeding Experimental Station, Sunndalsøra, is shown diagramatically in *Fig* 9. The system was designed to hold 100–150 thousand fish up to a weight of 2 g in eight $4\,m^2$ fibreglass tanks. Water flow through each tank is 30 l/min (litres per minute).

When water is re-circulated the fishes' metabolic products must be removed so that they do not accumulate to lethal levels, and oxygen used by the fish must be replaced. In the system shown in *Fig* 9 the sedimentation tank collects faeces and waste food from the fish tanks. In the biological filters, the construction of which is shown in *Fig* 10, bacterial action removes the nitrogenous metabolic products of the fish. The crushed limestone provides a surface on which these bacteria work and also maintains a stable water pH of 7.8. When starting up the system the biological filters are innoculated with a little garden soil to develop the proper bacterial culture. The sand filter removes small particles and bacteria greater than $1\,m\mu$ in diameter. The water heater is thermostatically controlled to provide the required water temperature. To re-oxygenate it the water falls through four perforated aluminium sheets, and this also serves to remove any nitrogen above saturation level. Ultra-violet light kills microbes smaller than $1\,m\mu$. Fresh water enters the head tank through a ball-valve to replace that removed with waste at the bottom of the sedimentation tank. Re-circulation saves water as well as power, and the system described here is estimated to use only about 10% of the water of a 'through flow' system for the same number of fish.

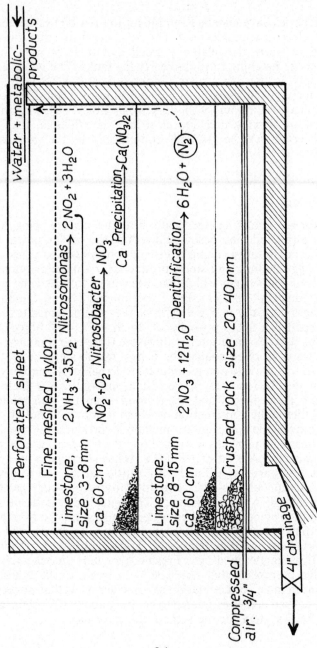

Fig 10. Diagram of the biological filter of a re-circulation system for smolt production. (From Risa and Skjervold, 1975).

24

Power station cooling water

A few units producing smolts or fingerlings are sited close to hydro-electric power stations which provide them with waste warm water at a comparatively low cost (*Fig* 11). All types of power stations use water for cooling their generators, but its quality is not always suitable for use in salmonid hatcheries. Coal burning power stations, for example, are frequently sited on polluted rivers and add chlorine to their water to reduce biological fouling of condensers. Nuclear stations normally use sea water for cooling. In Norway all power generation is by hydro-electric stations, but even these frequently pollute their cooling water with levels of copper which make it lethal to salmonids, so careful testing is necessary before its use is considered. The ideal situation is when a hatchery is planned as an integral part of a hydro power scheme, so that materials and techniques in building are used which ensure that the cooling water is not contaminated.

The temperature of power station cooling water cannot be controlled by the hatchery and is frequently over 10°C above ambient. Such water may be usable alone in winter, but at other times would be too hot for

Fig 11. A modern hatchery (left) built to take advantage of waste warm water from a hydro power station (right).

25

salmonids. In fish units using cooling water, therefore, it is usual to mix this with fresh water from other sources to obtain an optimal temperature for the eggs or fish. In salmon smolt production units sea water is also used, and by mixing warm fresh water, cold fresh water and sea water in different proportions a whole range of temperatures and salinities can be produced for supply to egg trays and fish tanks.

Supersaturation. Use of cooling water is not without problems, the most serious of which is supersaturation of the water with dissolved air. Solubility of both nitrogen and oxygen varies with temperature and pressure; the higher the atmospheric pressure and the colder the water the more dissolved gasses it will hold. Water entering a power station intake is normally approximately 100% saturated with air. Water reaches the power station *via* penstocks in which it is under pressure. When it is used to cool the generators its temperature rises rapidly and, although air tends to leave the water, unless it is sufficiently agitated the water can still retain too much air in solution. The concentration of air dissolved in the water is then not in equilibrium with the atmosphere at the new, higher water temperature. When this happens the water is said to be over 100% saturated with air, or supersaturated.

This is not important for the oxygen portion of the air, at least not at the degree of supersaturation usually encountered, but water which is saturated with nitrogen to around 107% or above can kill fish. The cause of death is the same as that in a diver with 'the bends'. After nitrogen is absorbed into the blood of the fish at a supersaturated level there is a tendency for its concentration to fall to the proper level of 100%. The result is that gaseous nitrogen comes out of solution in the blood and forms bubbles. These enter vessels in the vital organs and cause death. In fish afflicted in this way bubbles can be seen in small blood vessels in the gills, fins and elsewhere, and consequently this condition is often called 'gas bubble disease'.

To avoid mortalities due to supersaturation it is vital that power station cooling water is 'de-gassed' before being supplied to fish tanks. In Norway this is usually done by allowing it to fall through small holes in a series of stacked aluminium trays (*Fig* 12) before entering the mixing tanks. However, any system which exposes sufficient surface area of water to the air, so that the gas pressure can equilibrate with the atmosphere, would be adequate. A compact de-gassing system originally of American design but now used extensively in Sweden, and gaining popularity in Norway, is the so-called 'Inka' apparatus (*Fig* 13). This consists of a wooden box housing a perforated aluminium plate about 5 mm from its bottom. Incoming water enters by a slit at one end of the plate and flows in a thin layer on top of the plate from one end to the other, where it flows over a

Fig 12. Water is de-gassed as it falls through a stack of perforated aluminium plates.

weir and out of the apparatus. Air from a compressor is blown into the machine between the base of the box and the aluminium plate. It is then forced up through the holes in the plate, above which it comes into intimate contact with the film of water. The gas pressure of the water is then equilibrated with the air, which leaves the machine through a hole in the top of the box.

WATER QUALITY

pH

Neutral or slightly alkaline water is preferable for salmonid hatcheries,

27

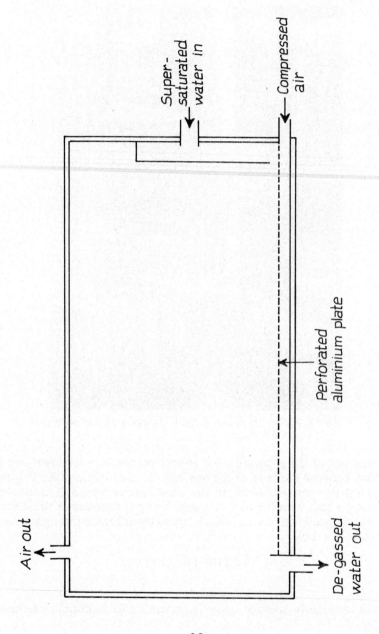

Fig 13. An "Inka" apparatus for de-gassing supersaturated water.

Super-saturated water in

Compressed air

Perforated aluminium plate

Air out

De-gassed water out

28

but any pH between about 6 and 8 is acceptable. Water pH above about 9 and below about 5.5 can kill fish, especially the sensitive egg and early fry stages of development. Some salmonid species are more sensitive to damage from low pH than others, and the order of susceptibility for the most common species appears to be rainbow trout>salmon>brown trout>brook trout.

The pH of many fresh waters in southern Norway has been dropping over the past few decades. The geological nature of the country is one reason for this. The underlying rocks are largely granite, gneisses and other hard rock types, with poor soil covering and very poor buffering capacity. Natural fresh waters are therefore poor in buffering ability, and incoming acid easily reduces their pH. A second reason is that much of the precipitation which falls on southern Norway is acidic. Rain with a pH as low as 3 has been recorded. The cause is atmospheric pollution, especially with sulphur dioxide, from the industrial areas of central Europe and Britain. The pollution is carried to Norway by the prevailing winds. The result is that hundreds of lakes and rivers now have a pH too low to support fish life, in some areas around pH 4. In many other waters the pH drops to dangerous levels seasonally, especially during the spring snow-melt, which is precisely the time when the sensitive eggs and newly-hatched fry of salmonids are present. Successful breeding becomes impossible in such waters (*Fig* 14) even though they may be able to support adult trout.

Acid pollution, which is getting worse each year, is important to fish culturists for two reasons. First, it means that in a large area of Norway the pH of fresh waters is too low for direct use in salmonid hatcheries. If it is essential to site a hatchery where it must use acidic water, this can be passed through a filter containing chalk to raise the pH before it is used for supplying egg trays or fish tanks. An alternative is to mix acid fresh water with sea water to give a salinity of up to about 6‰ as this serves to neutralize acidity. Second, it is useless for hatcheries to produce fish for re-stocking natural waters in which they have little chance of survival. The pH of some small lakes and spawning streams can be raised by adding chalk or lime, but this is expensive and impractical for large waters. Attempts are being made to selectively breed fish, especially brown trout, which are more tolerant to low pH (Gjedrem, 1976a).

Oxygen

Water entering salmonid hatcheries should, generally speaking, be 100% saturated with oxygen. If it is not, it should be made so by passing it through an aeration device, commonly a series of stacked perforated

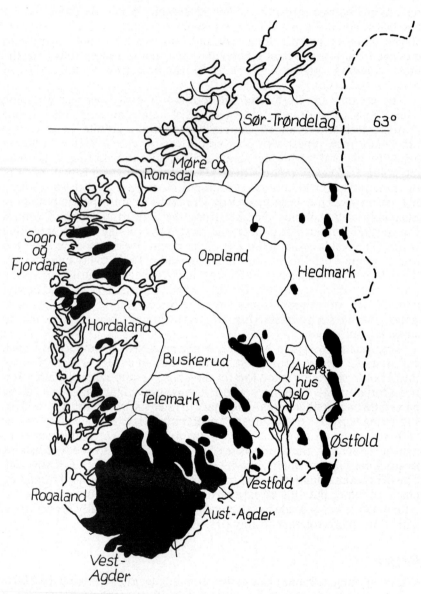

Fig 14. Areas of southern Norway in which salmonid populations are absent or reduced by acid water. Affected areas are shaded.

plates the same as is used to remove excess nitrogen. The concentration of oxygen in the water varies with temperature, but the outgoing water from a salmonid unit should never contain less than about 6 ppm (parts per million).

Metals

Copper ions can kill fish at concentrations as low as 0.02–0.04 mg/l; zinc at 0.4–0.5 mg/l. Natural waters with levels approaching these should be avoided. It is also essential that brass or copper pipes and fittings should not be used when installing plumbing in a hatchery. Iron frequently occurs in natural waters and can be precipitated onto the surface of eggs, where it hinders oxygen uptake and can cause suffocation. Concentrations of iron over about 0.5 mg/l are usually lethal.

Pollution

Water receiving pollutants of any kind should not be used in fish hatcheries. Norway generally has little industrial pollution compared with most European countries, but nevertheless local pollution from factories, the timber industry, and agriculture can be a problem. Apart from common pollutants which are lethal to fish, such as pesticides, detergents, chlorine and cyanide, several other substances taint the flesh of salmonids when present in sub-lethal concentrations. Among these are phenols, mineral oils, resins and tars. Where more than one pollutant occurs in the same water their effects on fish can be synergistic, so that fish can be killed even when no single pollutant is present in a lethal concentration.

Silt

The particle content of water is rarely high enough to kill large fish, but it can suffocate eggs and young fry. Extra work can also be produced by silting up of ponds or tanks. Waters which are frequently prone to high silt content should therefore be avoided. However, where a little occurs in a water supply it can be removed with a rapid sand filter.

WATER SOURCE AND QUANTITY

It is generally better to have water supplied to a hatchery by gravity flow rather than by pumps. This is partly for economic reasons: electric pumps use power which costs money, and partly for security reasons: a gravity supply is less likely to break down than a pumped one. If electric pumps are relied on for water supply there must always be a back-up system of diesel pumps or generators in case of electricity failure.

Gravity supply is often possible from surface waters, ie lakes, rivers or streams, and in these the intakes to the hatchery pipeline must be screened to avoid taking in debris or wild fish. The screens must be placed in such a way that they do not become blocked by ice or debris. The disadvantages of surface water for use in hatcheries are the wide fluctuations in temperature and water flow, and their liability to flooding with its consequent increase in water turbidity. Springs frequently have a more constant water flow but the temperature, though stable, is usually lower than that of surface water in summer so that fish will grow less well.

Sub-surface water usually has to be pumped. It sometimes contains high levels of metals and other undesirable ions and has little oxygen but it is free of silt. Temperature, usually fairly constant over the year, is higher than that of surface water in winter and lower in summer. When it is necessary to pump surface waters up to the hatchery, the intake should be placed under a thick layer of stones and gravel. This acts as a filter to prevent debris entering the pump. Care must be taken to ensure that intakes cannot suck in air, otherwise supersaturation problems can result.

For smolt units, sea water is also required. This is usually pumped through a screened inlet from 30 or 40 m down in a fjord. At that depth the water is clean and relatively free from suspended matter and the planktonic stages of development of marine organisms, eg mussels, which could otherwise foul pipes and tanks. The water temperature also remains considerably higher in winter than it does in the surface layers of the sea.

It can be seen that all sources of water have both advantages and disadvantages. Most large units producing young salmonids are provided with water from several different sources. This is not only for security in the event of breakdown in any one supply but also so that by mixing different waters a range of temperatures and salinities can be produced at different times of year according to the unit's requirements.

Flow rate

The amount of water required varies greatly according to its temperature, the type of tanks, raceways or ponds used, and the species and size of fish grown.

In general, rainbow trout have a higher oxygen demand than salmon, and therefore require more water. Small fish need more water per kilo than larger ones. Computer curves of water requirement for different sizes of fish at different temperature for both species have been produced by Skjervold (1973) from the formulae of Liao (1971). As examples, two of the curves for salmon are shown in *Fig 15.*

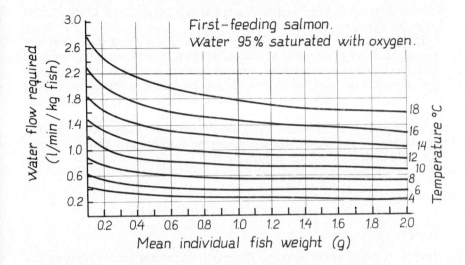

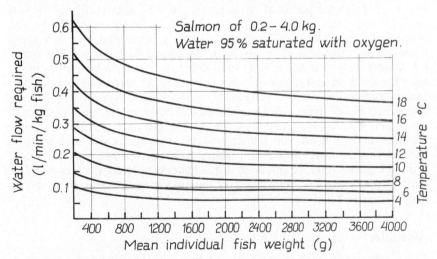

Fig 15. Water flow requirement for salmon of different sizes at different temperatures. (*From Skjervold, 1973*).

33

Senstad (1975) calculated that a unit using 'Swedish' type plastic tanks to produce 100 thousand smolts per year would require a minimum of 5,000–7,000 l/min if it produced one-year-old smolts, and a minimum of 6,000–8,000 l/min if it produced two-year-old smolts. An extra 60–70 l/min is also needed for supply to egg hatching trays, and 1,000–1,500 l/min for the early fry tanks.

The volume of water required increases as its oxygen content decreases, and oxygen content at saturation decreases as water temperature rises. In surface waters the flow rate also tends to be lowest at the warmest time of year. Volume of water available at the warmest, driest time of year must therefore be taken as the measure of how much the source can supply.

When planning a new unit, a site should be selected where considerably more water is available than the minimum immediately thought necessary. This allows for later expansion.

OTHER SITE REQUIREMENTS

Access

Next to a good water supply, the most important factor limiting the suitability of sites for fresh water salmonid units in Norway is accessibility. Apart from the personal requirements of staff, foodstuffs for the fish must be delivered regularly to ensure freshness, and young fish must be transported out. Much of Norway is sparsely populated. In many areas there is no railway, and it would be necessary to build a track many kilometres long from the nearest road. Even then it might be impossible to keep the track open because of heavy snowfalls in winter. Units producing smolts must usually be located near the coast so that they can pump in sea water. Access to these units is often easiest by boat, and they frequently have their own quay. Generally, the further the unit is situated from a harbour or rail head, the higher will be transport costs and the less competitive the unit will be with others more conveniently placed. Legal rights of access must be obtained if it is necessary to cross other people's land to reach the site, and rights of land tenure and water use must be properly arranged.

Amenities

The same considerations apply to other amenities. Electricity supply is needed for water heaters, automatic feeders and pumps, and to allow civilized living conditions for staff. A telephone is essential for ordering supplies, arranging sales of fish, and summoning veterinary or other specialist help in an emergency. The manager should live nearby, or preferably at the unit, to be on hand in case of emergencies such as water supply failure and to deter theft of fish or equipment.

4 Smolt and Fingerling Production

PRODUCTION OF EGGS

Brood stock

The ideal source of brood stock varies according to the purpose for which the offspring are to be reared. If smolts or fingerlings are being produced for release into natural waters it is satisfactory to capture brood fish from rivers or the sea, strip them of eggs and sperm, and return them to the wild. The genetic composition of the young fish reared for release will then be the same as at least part of the wild population into which they will return. However, when fish are to be grown right through from the egg to maturity or slaughter in captivity it is highly desirable to breed selectively using brood fish which show characteristics wanted by the farmer or consumer. For this purpose selected stocks must be kept in captivity for many generations, so that gradual improvements made by selection are perpetuated and the genetic composition of the captive stock will gradually diverge from the wild one from which it was originally derived. So far little progress has been made in the selective breeding of salmonids, but this field has great potential for improving fish farm yields in the future (Chapter 12).

Using captive stocks of fish to provide eggs also lessens disease risks. Several serious virus diseases can be transmitted with eggs, and most governments require certification that both the fish farm and the stock of fish the eggs are taken from have been free of these diseases for several generations before they will allow import of eggs. This certification obviously cannot be given to wild fish and, aside from the legal restraints, any fish farmer who takes in eggs from an undocumented source risks introducing serious disease to his farm.

At present, brood stock for all rainbow trout farmed in Norway are taken from captive stocks, since this species does not spawn naturally in this country. Most salmon whose offspring are to be reared to large size in captivity are also taken from captive stocks. These fish can be used to provide eggs or sperm again two years later, but this is not common. Their survival after stripping in captivity is frequently over 70%, much higher than after wild spawning. Some salmon brood stock are still taken from the wild, and these are stripped only once and then released.

As already stressed (Chapter 2), salmon must be harvested before the onset of sexual maturity. Time taken to reach sexual maturity is in part genetically determined, and fish from some stocks habitually become grilse, *ie* attain sexual maturity after only one year in the sea. It is vital, therefore, that if salmon brood stock must be obtained by capture from the wild, grilse rivers are strictly avoided.

Stripping and fertilization

Whether salmon brood stock are transferred to fresh water before stripping, or are stripped direct from sea water, is entirely according to the preference of the individual fish farmer. Fish to be transferred to fresh water are usually moved from their sea pens about a month before stripping. The same type of boat is used for their transport as described below for transport of smolts and fingerlings. The brood fish are gradually acclimatized to fresh water through several intermediate salinities. This process is reversed after stripping, when the salmon are gradually acclimatized back to sea water over two or three weeks. They are then transported by boat back to the sea unit.

Rainbow trout can also be stripped direct from sea water, but in practice they are almost always transferred to fresh water or water of low salinity the autumn before they become fully mature, or kept in such water permanently. This avoids the very high mortality associated with maturation in the sea. After gradual acclimatization to fresh water, and stripping for the first time, rainbow trout brood stock are kept permanently in this water and not returned to the sea. Often water of low salinity is used instead of pure fresh water to ensure that brood fish remain free of fungal infection.

Brown trout and other fresh water species cultured to re-stock natural waters are, of course, kept permanently in fresh water.

Ripe females can be recognized by their distended but soft bellies, their swollen and reddened vents and, when quite ready for stripping, by the fact that eggs are easily expelled by pressing the belly. Mature male salmon, brown trout and char develop a hooked lower jaw, and all male fish are ready for stripping when milt can be expelled by pressure on the belly. Males frequently become fully mature earlier than females.

37

Stripping is made much easier if the fish are anaesthetized. MS 222 used to be popular in Norway, but now chlorobutanol ($C_4H_7Cl_3O$) is normally used. This is made up with a little 70% alcohol and then added to a tank of water to give a concentration of about 8–10 mg/l. Brood fish placed in this water become quiet very quickly.

Fertilization is by the dry method. It is important to ensure that the eggs and sperm do not come into contact with water before they are well mixed together. This is because water causes eggs to swell and become impervious to penetration by sperm, and sperm to quickly become inactive and incapable of fertilizing the eggs. Many workers gently wipe the brood fish with a towel to remove surface water immediately after taking them from the anaesthetic bath.

Eggs from female fish are expelled into a plastic bowl by firmly stroking the belly backwards towards the vent (*Fig* 16), and milt from male fish is expelled in a similar manner onto the eggs. The eggs and sperm are well mixed together either with the fingers or a soft implement such as a brush or feather (*Fig* 17), and left for a few minutes for fertilization to take place. Newly stripped eggs and sperms are sensitive to light, and should be shaded from direct sunlight. After standing, a little water is added to the bowl and poured off to remove excess milt. When this process has been repeated several times the eggs can be put into water

Fig 16. Stripping eggs from a mature salmon. (*Photograph: Vidar Vassvik*).

38

Fig 17. Mixing milt with salmon eggs to effect fertilization.
(Photograph: Vidar Vassvik).

and left for an hour or two to 'harden', during which time they take up water and swell. Alternatively the fertilized eggs can be put straight into the hatching trays after washing.

The number of female brood fish stripped into the bowl at one time, and the number of males used to provide milt to fertilize their eggs, vary according to the farmer's habit. However, it is usual to strip several females together. Although each male produces millions of sperm, sufficient to fertilize the eggs of many females, it is customary to use milt from at least two males on each batch of eggs in case a sterile male is encountered. An overall mating ratio of four or five females to one male is about average.

Transport of eggs and milt

Eggs of salmon stripped and fertilized at a sea unit can safely be transported in water, after hardening, to incubators in a fresh water unit for hatching. Alternatively, eggs and milt can be stripped into separate plastic containers at the sea unit, transported immediately to the hatchery, and fertilized there. Provided that they are not allowed to come into contact with water, the eggs and sperm will stay alive separately for at least 24 hours. Milt or eggs, either fertilized or unfertilized, should be kept in ice-cooled containers for long journeys.

HATCHING

Incubating systems

Several different types of egg incubator are used in Norway.

Troughs. The simplest is a longitudinal trough along which water flows from end to end. A few centimetres depth of water is maintained by a sill near the downstream end of the trough, and water passes out to waste through a vertical pipe in the bottom of the trough downstream of the sill. Troughs can be home-made of wood to any convenient size, but commercially manufactured ones of fibreglass are frequently 40 cm wide and 220 or 360 cm long. Eggs are spread over the bottom of the trough, sometimes on a layer of gravel, and the water passes in a stream over them.

The same type of fibreglass trough fitted with commercially made hatching trays is the most popular incubator system in Norway, the most common being manufactured by the Swedish company Astra-Ewos A/B. A 220 cm trough holds four, and a 360 cm trough seven, hatching trays or boxes, and the water level in the trough is maintained by a vertical standpipe at the downstream end (*Fig* 18). Each fibreglass tray has lips around its top edges, which at the sides are supported by the edges of the trough. The bottom of each tray is of perforated aluminium on which the eggs are spread, and this lies about 3 cm above the bottom of the trough. The downstream vertical side of each tray extends down to the bottom of the hatching trough, whilst near its top is a wide slit covered with a perforated aluminium sheet, through which water passes out of the tray. Water flowing in at the upstream end of the trough passes under the first tray, up through the aluminium sheet at its bottom, past the eggs, and then out through the aluminium screen in the downstream side of the tray. The same pattern is repeated at the next tray, and so on down the trough, so that the water passes through every box in the trough and then out through

Fig 18. "California" type hatching trough and trays. (*Photograph: Norsk Landbrukskjemi A/S—Astra-Ewos A/B*).

the standpipe. This incubator system is often referred to as the 'California' system.

Sometimes, specially made systems in which the water passes downwards past the eggs are used. These are again based on horizontal troughs holding egg trays, but water is supplied to each tray individually from plastic pipes running longitudinally above the troughs. The aluminium plate in the bottom of each tray is perforated with slits instead of round holes, so that eggs are retained but newly-hatched fry are able to pass down through it. Water enters the top of each tray, runs down past the eggs, through the aluminium plate and out through a screen in the side of the tray into the trough, and flows to waste.

'Battery' systems. A number of commercially manufactured battery systems are available. These basically consist of hatching trays, similar to California ones in that the water passes up past the eggs, but these are stacked vertically one on top of the other instead of horizontally. Each egg tray is held in its own outer container, into which water flows from above. The water then goes up through the base of the inner container, past the eggs, and out, either through a central screened pipe or through

41

perforations at the edge of the container, into a pipe which carries it down into the side of the next tray below. The outer trays fit into frames like drawers in a chest-of-drawers, and may be stacked as many as 16 high from floor to ceiling. Battery systems are popular in the USA but are not much used in Norway.

Merits of different incubators. Troughs in all incubator systems which use them are generally placed at about waist-height for ease of access, and side-by-side in pairs as access is only necessary to one side of each trough. Battery systems take up far less space, but to inspect eggs it is necessary to pull out the drawers, thus disturbing the eggs. It is also inconvenient to inspect drawers at different heights, and with a high stack much climbing and kneeling is necessary. Even with trough systems, however, many hatcheries mount several troughs on frames one above the other to accommodate more eggs in the available floor area (*Fig* 19), and this also makes egg inspection and handling less convenient.

Battery systems also use less water per thousand eggs than troughs but, except in units specializing in the production of millions of eggs for sale, the water requirements of eggs are very low compared with those of the young fish in the rest of the farm. Therefore, if it is necessary to save water at the egg stage, it could be argued that the whole unit has been established on an insufficient water supply.

Fig 19. Stacked hatching troughs.

The quality of water becomes poorer as it passes more eggs so, from this point of view, systems in which each egg tray receives a separate supply are best and battery systems worst. In the simplest trough system without egg trays the water flow around the eggs is not as good as in other systems.

Silos. Some companies produce millions of eggs more than they need to provide themselves with young fish, and sell the surplus eggs when they become eyed. To incubate large numbers of eggs to this stage of development 'silos', *ie* upright plastic cylinders containing egg baskets, are often used. Each silo holds about 25 l of eggs, but requires only 8 l/min of water. Water enters the silo at the bottom, flows up past the eggs, and leaves at the top of the container. Because such a small amount of water is required, it costs little to heat in order to speed egg development. This apparatus is of course not comparable with the hatching systems described earlier, as if fish were allowed to hatch in it they would die.

Volume of eggs. Large female fish usually produce bigger eggs than small ones, and egg size also varies between fish species. It is usual to measure fertilized eggs by volume before putting them into their hatching trays, and each litre will contain 4–5,000 salmon eggs, 5–10,000 brown or rainbow trout eggs, or 12–15,000 Arctic char eggs. Each California type hatching tray will comfortably hold about 1.5 l of eggs, and for these water flow should be about 8 l/min for a trough holding four trays, or 12 l/min for seven trays.

Development of eggs

The rate at which eggs develop depends on their species and the temperature of the water they are kept in. It is usual to measure development time in day-degrees, *ie* number of days after fertilization multiplied by water temperature ($^\circ$C) over the period. Eggs actually take fewer day-degrees to develop to a given stage at very low temperatures, but approximate development times at normal hatchery temperature (about 8°C), together with other hatchery data for the common Norwegian salmonid species, are shown in *Table* 1. Salmon eggs, for example, become eyed after about 245 day-degrees. At this stage of development the eggs are most resistant to handling, and can be transported for long distances if required. Eggs which are bought and sold therefore normally change hands at this time. Salmon eggs may hatch after about 510 day-degrees. If the hatchery can control the water temperature, therefore, rate of development of eggs can be adjusted so that they will hatch earlier than under natural conditions or at the most convenient time. Those units with access to hydro-electric power station cooling water frequently maintain their eggs in water at about 8°C, and this can bring forward the hatching of salmon eggs to the beginning of January, instead of the beginning of May without heating. In units without warm power-station water electric water heating is sometimes available. This can either be used in the same way as cooling water, or only to synchronize hatching of different batches of eggs, *eg* to speed hatching of eggs stripped in December the previous year so that they hatch at about the same time as eggs taken in October. Rainbow trout eggs develop faster than salmon, often requiring only about 370 day-degrees from fertilization to hatching. With heated water, rainbow trout eggs stripped in January can be hatched at the end of February. For spring-stripped rainbow trout eggs natural water temperatures are high enough to induce rapid hatching.

Table 1. Development statistics for salmonids cultured at the Fish Breeding Experimental Station, Sunndalsøra, Norway.

Species	Date of stripping	Diameter of eggs (mm)	Development time (day-degrees at 8°C)			% one year old 'smolts'
			To eyed egg	To hatch	From hatch to first-feeding	
Atlantic salmon	20 Oct–12 Dec	6.2	245	510	290	75
Rainbow trout	10 Jan–1 Mar	5.1	175	370	150	95
Sea trout	15 Oct–1 Nov	5.2	240	500	280	80
Migratory char	10 Oct–1 Nov	4.3	220	445	225	90
Pink salmon	20 Sep–1 Oct	7.6	280	640	290	100

Hatchery work

Dead eggs. Apart from checking the water supply and keeping the trays and troughs clean, the most important job while eggs are incubating is the regular removal of dead eggs. These can be recognized because they turn white due to coagulation of the yolk. Fungal spores are usually present in the water, and if dead eggs are not removed fungus will quickly grow on them and perhaps spread to infect live eggs. In most Norwegian hatcheries dead eggs are removed by hand, using either a simple siphon tube or a rubber suction bulb attached to a glass tube. However, for units incubating a lot of eggs, machines are available which will separate dead and live eyed eggs automatically. Eggs are poured into a hopper at the top and individually pass a photo-electric cell. Live eggs pass through into one bucket, and dead eggs are diverted into another.

When some of the eggs have reached the eyed stage of development it is

44

customary to 'shock' them by jerking their trays or tipping them into a bucket. Those eggs which were not fertilized, or have since died but have not turned white, will then do so and can be separated easily. Mortality of eggs after the eyed stage is usually slight.

To reduce labour, the managers of some hatcheries prefer to control fungal infection of eggs by chemical treatment instead of by removing dead eggs regularly. Malachite green is normally used, and this can be made up into a 0.25% solution, 100 ml of which is added to the upstream end of each hatching trough every two or three days. Alternatively, lower concentrations can be used for longer periods by allowing a continuous drip of solution to run into the trough.

Counting eggs. Eggs are sold by number, so in units specializing in the sale of eggs it is essential to be able to count eggs accurately, and the manager of any unit needs to know approximately how many young fish he must plan for. Exact counting is done with a special perspex plate in which a known number, often 200, of holes are drilled. The holes are countersunk to such a diameter that one egg fits perfectly in each. By slipping the plate under a batch of eggs and removing it, exactly 200 eggs are taken each time (*Fig* 20). However, this is rather laborious where large

Fig 20. Counting salmonid eggs using a special perspex plate. (*Photograph: Arne Kittelsen*).

45

Fig 21. Measuring egg diameter with a V-scale. (*Photograph: Arne Kittelsen*).

numbers of eggs are involved, and slightly less accurate methods are usually resorted to. Frequently a special V-shaped 25 cm rule is used (*Fig 21*). Eggs are lined up touching one another in the bottom of the V, and the number required to fill the scale counted, thus giving a measure of egg diameter. A table giving the volume occupied by a given number of eggs of that diameter is then consulted, and subsequently any number of eggs required is measured by volume. Mean egg diameters for several salmonid species are included in Table 1. A reasonably accurate estimate of egg number can also be obtained by knowing the speed of operation of the photo-electric sorting devices described above, which frequently handle around 100 thousand eggs per hour.

FRY AND FINGERLINGS

Newly hatched fry are left in their egg trays for a few weeks, but the water supply is increased because their oxygen demand is about double that of eggs. During this time the fry do not move much. Neither do they eat, but obtain nourishment from their yolk sacs which contain the remains of the food supplies from the egg. How long the fry take to absorb most of the yolk sac and be ready to start feeding depends on water temperature.

46

Salmon require about 290 day-degrees (Table 1), *ie* 4–5 weeks at 8°C, from hatch to the time they are ready to start taking external food. When yolk sacs are about two thirds absorbed, and the young fish start swimming about, they are normally transferred to tanks to begin feeding, but some units 'first-feed' the fry while still in the egg trays or troughs.

Fry

First-feeding. The period when fry must change over from drawing nourishment from the yolk sac to feeding for themselves is probably the most critical for the culturist, and heavy losses can occur at this time. Salmon are much more difficult to first-feed than rainbow trout, and up to 50% mortality of salmon at this stage is not uncommon.

Salmon require a water temperature of 8–9°C before they will start to feed. This is no problem for units using hydro-electric power station cooling water, and they can first-feed their fish in January-February even though natural fresh water temperature at that time may be near 0°C. Units using surface or cold spring water are also alright, as the eggs will not hatch until at least April, and the fry will not be ready to start feeding before May-June, by which time the natural water temperatures are high enough. Units using ground or spring water with a winter temperature of a few degrees celsius can have the worst problems. Here, development of

Fig 22. Rows of fibreglass tanks for salmonid fry. (*Photograph: Department of Animal Genetics and Breeding, Agricultural University of Norway*).

47

eggs over the winter will be faster, and hatch will be earlier, than under natural conditions. The fry may therefore be ready to start feeding before the surface fresh water temperatures are high enough and, unless the ground water can be heated a few degrees, this will not be warm enough either. The fish will then die after using up their yolk sacs.

Fry tanks. Fry are kept indoors, generally in small (1–4 m²) glassfibre tanks holding about 25 cm depth of water (*Fig* 22), the most popular type being manufactured by Astra-Ewos A/B. This same type of tank is frequently used for young salmon right through their fresh water development until they are ready to smolt and be acclimatized to sea water. Some of these tanks are circular, but even the most widely used square ones have rounded corners so that when the water enters tangentially a circulating current is established around each tank. The supply of water to each tank can be individually regulated by a tap. In the centre of each tank is a rectangular aluminium screen through which water leaves. Water level is regulated either by an external standpipe arrangement (*Fig* 23), or by a simple elbow pipe in the same position. The standpipe is removable and fitted with a handle at the top so that it can be pulled out to empty the tank.

Fig 23. A circulating-type glassfibre tank with external standpipe. (*Photograph: Norsk Landbrukskjemi A/S—Astra-Ewos A/B*).

Alternatively, elbow pipes can be turned down to one side.

Water circulation in the tanks tends to wash waste food, faeces and dead fish into the centre, and as the fish grow larger the size of perforation in the drain screen can be increased to allow larger particles to leave of their own accord. Thus these tanks are said to be partially self-cleaning. However, small particles tend to coagulate on the screen, and it is necessary to assist tank flushing manually. This is done without removing the fish by swirling the water around the tank with a brush, removing the standpipe thus creating strong suction down onto the screen, and brushing over the screen to help particles through. Live fish tend to keep out of the way, but dead ones are sucked onto the screen and are removed manually. Regular cleaning is essential, otherwise fungus will develop on dead fish and waste, and decaying organic matter may use up much of the oxygen in the water.

Water circulation also serves to spread food around the tank, and fish orientate themselves against the current as they would in a natural stream. Commercially produced dry food is given to excess by automatic feeders (Chapter 8).

Stocking density. First-feeding fry can be kept fairly densely crowded. Some studies have shown that mortality of young salmon fry is actually lower at high density (Refstie and Kittelsen, 1976), though the reason for this is not clear. Up to about 10,000 individuals per square metre of tank can be safely accommodated. Current around the tank should not be greater than the fish can comfortably swim against.

After they have started to take food and begun to grow, the fish are transferred into other tanks. In many units these are of the same type as the first-feeding tanks, so that fish are simply being thinned out to give them more space to grow. In units where they were first-fed in their hatching troughs, however, the fry are often transferred directly into larger growing tanks where they will stay for the rest of their fresh water lives.

It is known that crowding depresses growth of salmon parr and rainbow trout fingerlings (*eg* Refstie and Kittelsen, 1976; Refstie, 1977). Stocking density in fry tanks is therefore frequently restricted to around 25 kg of fish per cubic metre of water, and the growing fry are graded to ensure that all fish in any one tank are of approximately the same size. This is done to avoid cannibalism which often occurs when large and small fish share the same tank, especially with rainbow trout. It is also easier to select a size of food pellet suitable for all individuals in a tank if the fish are of uniform size. Water flow through fry tanks is frequently about one litre/min/kg of fish.

Rainbow trout are sometimes first-fed in indoor concrete or wood raceways, long narrow troughs through which water flows from end to end. In newer units these are being replaced by fibreglass tanks.

Growing tanks

In Norway, salmon parr are frequently kept indoors in fibreglass tanks right through the first summer's growth (*Fig* 22). Alternatively they may be moved to larger, outdoor containers, and this is usually done with rainbow trout fingerlings. Though a wide variety of different types of tanks and ponds are used in this country, generally speaking salmon parr are grown in square or round enclosures with circulating water, whereas rainbow trout are grown in raceways or ponds with a longitudinal flow. This is not a hard-and-fast rule, however, and some people use circulating tanks for trout or, more rarely, raceways for salmon.

Circular tanks or ponds work on the same principle as fry tanks with water entering tangentially and circulation washing waste into a central drain. These tanks can be of any size, and between three and ten metres diameter is common. Small tanks are usually commercially made of fibreglass (*Fig* 24). Large ones are specially made on site from reinforced concrete or concrete blocks covered with a layer of cement and water-proofed with epoxy resin paint (*Fig* 25). They are built above ground and

Fig 24. Square fibreglass growing tanks for salmonids. (*Photograph: Lars Bull-Berg*).

50

Fig 25. 10 metre diameter circular concrete tanks for smolt production. (*Photograph: Arne Kittelsen*).

Fig 26. Small concrete raceways for rainbow trout. (*Photograph: Lars Bull-Berg*).

51

inside them their bottoms slope slightly down towards the centre, where the outlet screen is situated. Under the screen is a concrete sump, and from this a wide pipe runs under the pond to a standpipe arrangement to one side of it, by which the water level is regulated and which can be removed to empty the pond. Large circular fibreglass tanks sometimes have standpipes in the centre of the tank instead of outside, and these are screened at the top. This system is less convenient as it does not have such an efficient self-cleaning action.

Fig 27. Large concrete raceways for salmon smolt production. (*Photograph: A/S Mowi*).

Young rainbow trout are sometimes grown in earth ponds of the type described in Chapter 2. As a precaution against whirling disease (*Myxosoma cerebralis*) trout are not stocked into earth ponds until they are over about 5 cm in length and calcification of the cranium is complete, when this protozoan parasite can no longer attack them. Concrete raceways (*Figs* 26 and 27) are in use in a number of units, but are not as popular as in the USA. In Norway, fish farmers tend to prefer circulating tanks.

Stocking densities and water flows vary according to the design of the growing enclosure and practice of the individual farmer. As an example, a circular concrete pond of 10 m diameter and about 1 m water depth will comfortably hold about 20,000 salmon up to the smolt stage of development, or 1,500 kg of rainbow trout, with 600 l/min throughput of water.

Outdoor tanks, raceways or ponds containing small fish are usually covered with nylon nets to exclude birds or other predators. Netting of a mesh size big enough so that it does not catch snow must be used in winter, otherwise it will be pushed down into the water and could entangle fish. Smaller tanks are sometimes fitted with fibreglass lids which, apart from excluding predators, shelter the fish from excess light and outside disturbance (*Fig* 28). Holes in the lids admit sufficient light for the fish to feed by.

Fig 28. Lidded circular fibreglass tanks for smolt production. (*Photograph: A/S Mowi*).

E

Routine work

Cleaning. Apart from feeding, which is described in Chapter 8, the most frequent job is cleaning of tanks. Fry tanks are cleaned as described above at least once a week, and each tank has its own brush to lessen the chances of transferring disease organisms from one tank to another. When a tank is emptied of fish it can be given a more thorough scrubbing to remove algal growth, and be disinfected with formalin at a concentration of about 1:3,000 before new fish are put into it. Large ponds and raceways are cleaned less frequently, but should be completely drained, scrubbed and disinfected each year after their fish have gone.

Enclosures which receive brackish or sea water for part of the year require painting about every two years with a copper-based anti-fouling paint to inhibit the growth of sedentary marine organisms which enter in their planktonic stages of development. The paint is poisonous to fish, so after being left for a day to dry the tank must be flushed with clean water for three or four days before any fish are introduced.

Grading. Young fish are usually graded by size several times during their fresh water growth. This is often done using a rectangular open-topped box, the bottom of which is composed of bars. The bars, made of

Fig 29. Size-grading young fish. (*Photograph: Vidar Vassvik*).

54

Fig 30. Grading apparatus for salmonids. (*Photograph: Norsk Landbrukskjemi A/S— Astra-Ewos A/B*).

plastic tubes of about 1 cm diameter, are spaced a given distance apart, and the bottom of the box is removable so that grids of differently-spaced bars can be substituted. Fish are put into the box, which is moved backwards and forwards so that individuals less than the width of the gap between the bars will fall through, whilst those bigger are retained in the box (*Fig 29*).

For grading large numbers of fish, faster sorting machines are commercially available (*Fig 30*). Basically, these machines consist of a sloping 'table' composed of longitudinal bars. The bars are not quite parallel, the gap between them being smaller at the top of the table and widening towards the bottom. At the extreme top end of the table is an open-bottomed box, and underneath the grading table there is room for three fish tanks. In use, fish taken from a growing tank or pond are poured into the box at the top end of the table. They pass out of the bottom of this box by gravity, and each fish slides down on top of the bars until it reaches a part of the table where the space between adjacent bars is wide enough for it to fall through, when it drops into one of the tanks below the table. The

55

Fig 31. Herding fish into a small space for removal by dip net. (*Photograph: Arne Kittelsen*).

fish are thus graded into three size groups.

It is easy to catch fish for grading, or to weigh samples to estimate average size, from small tanks by using a dip net. To catch fish in large tanks or raceways the water level is first drawn down and a moveable screen which fits across the width of the enclosure is used to herd the fish into a small space (*Fig* 31) from where they can be removed easily with dip nets. The moveable screens are frequently made from a wood, galvanized steel tube, or aluminium framework, covered with fine-meshed nylon netting.

Water quality measurements. Routine measurements of dissolved oxygen concentration at the outlet of all tanks should be made at intervals, and water flow adjusted accordingly. Excellent oxygen probes which give a direct reading are commercially available, but meter readings should be checked against standard Winkler titrations at intervals. Where heated water is used, it is vital to check dissolved nitrogen concentration in the incoming water at frequent intervals, preferably daily. Easy-to-use instruments are now available to measure total gas saturation, and nitrogen concentration is calculated or read from tables taking into account the

56

oxygen concentration, barometric pressure and temperature.

Frequent visual inspection of fish is very important. Experienced workers can often tell not only when anything is wrong but when anything is likely to go wrong by simply observing the behaviour of the fish, especially during feeding.

ACCLIMATIZATION TO SEA WATER

Physiological changes

The change from fresh to salt water life is a drastic one for young salmonids. The salt concentration in the body fluids of salmonids is slightly higher when in sea water than in fresh water, but is always in between that of fresh and sea water itself. When a fish lives in fresh water, therefore, the process of osmosis tends to draw water into its body, mainly across the gills but also through the alimentary canal. The fish must constantly get rid of excess water by producing a large flow of dilute urine. In sea water, on the other hand, the tendency is for water to be drawn out of the fish's body. This is overcome by drinking sea water, but unfortunately this means that a lot of unwanted salt is ingested too. The excess salt is excreted through special cells in the gills.

A fish transferred from fresh to sea water, therefore, must reverse its fluid control mechanisms, and this physiological change takes time. Under natural conditions the young fish themselves can determine when they will enter the sea. The fish can also determine the rate of transition from fresh to sea water by taking advantage of the intermediate salinities occurring in estuaries, where young fish may loiter for several days. However, under artificial conditions of rearing in fish farms the culturist must make these decisions for the fish, which may die if he transfers them to sea water prematurely or too suddenly.

Salmon. As mentioned in Chapter 2, Atlantic salmon undergo a physiological pre-adaptation to sea water by smolting. Smoltification occurs in spring. Smolts kept in fresh water will often de-smoltify back to parr and, if they survive, turn into smolts again the next spring. Size is the main factor determining at what age salmon will smolt. By increasing the temperature of the water in which the fish are kept, and by optimal feeding and general husbandry, some smolt production units in Norway are able to induce 50–75% of their fish to smolt at one year old, *ie* in the spring of their second year, and the rest smolt at two years of age. It is important to note that the critical size for smoltification must be reached by the right time of year. If a fish is not quite big enough to smolt by May or June of one year it must wait a whole year until the next spring before it gets another chance, regardless of what size it reaches in the intervening months. Minimum size at which salmon will smolt can be as low as 15 g, but it depends on genetic and environmental factors. Mean size of one-year-old smolts is about 30 g. Larger smolts are preferred as they are thought to have a better chance of survival and good growth in sea water, and they therefore command a higher price (Chapter 10).

Rainbow trout. Though one sea-going race of the same species, called steelhead trout, does smolt, the rainbow trout does not. Nevertheless it does readily adapt to life in sea water. Rainbow trout above about 50 g in weight can usually tolerate direct transfer to sea water and, unlike salmon, once over the minimum size rainbow trout can be transferred to sea water at any time of year.

Acclimatization

Most commonly, salmon smolts are not transferred direct from fresh to sea water in Norway, but are acclimatized gradually through several intermediate salinities, sometimes over several months. Rainbow trout are also sometimes treated in this way, but sometimes transferred directly with no prior acclimatization. However, in Norway it is impossible to separate acclimatization to sea water from the question of overcoming low winter water temperature, which is the dominating consideration right through the production cycle for salmonids in this country. It is economically highly desirable, for the reasons given in Chapter 2, to produce a high percentage of one-year-old salmon smolts, and this cannot be done if the fish are kept over the winter in fresh water at natural, low temperatures.

Units having plenty of cheap warm water from hydro-electric power stations can speed the growth of their salmon parr or rainbow trout fingerlings over the winter by maintaining the fresh water temperature at 10 or 12°C. They are not obliged to use sea water over the winter, and acclimatization of fish to sea water need not start until early spring. Where salmon parr are grown in indoor 'fry' tanks over the first summer, however, fish which will smolt at one year old are graded out from the rest in autumn and winter and moved to outdoor tanks or ponds ready for acclimatization. Each hatchery manager must learn by experience to recognize at what size his fish will smolt. At the Fish Breeding Experimental Station, Sunndalsøra, for example, over 90% of parr which will not pass a 10 mm grader in February or before will smolt in May of the same year. Acclimatization to sea water at Sunndalsøra begins in April, when salinity of the water supply to outdoor tanks is raised to 15‰. During the first two weeks of May salinity is gradually increased to full sea water (32‰). Fish are held in full sea water for at least a week before transport.

Smolt production units without a cheap supply of warm fresh water often increase water salinity much earlier to take advantage of the higher winter temperature of deep-sea water. Salinity frequently starts at about 6‰ in October-November and is gradually increased over winter to a maximum of 25–32 ‰ by the following May. In this way a sufficiently high temperature is maintained for fish growth to continue over winter and a high percentage of one-year-old smolts is produced.

To obtain sea water of a suitable quality, and of a temperature which does not fall below 6–8°C in winter, it must be pumped from deep in a fjord. This is done by electric pumps and, in case of electricity failure, a back-up system of diesel pumps or generators must be available. Mixing tanks and complicated plumbing to allow blending of sea and fresh waters to produce the required salinities are also necessary. All this equipment and power is expensive and adds considerably to the cost of smolt production. However, without pumped sea water in winter many units would be unable to induce a significant percentage of their fish to smolt at one year old without heating water electrically. It is possible that in the future re-circulation systems may make the use of electrically-heated water more economical, but compared with the costs of installing such systems the provision of a pumped supply of sea water is cheap.

Acclimatizing fish to sea water gradually has several other advantages over direct transfer. First, when transferred to sea units for on-growing, mortalities of fish treated in this way are lower than those transferred directly. Secondly, direct transfer is a big physiological shock. Fish treated in this way frequently do not feed for days or even weeks after transfer, thus reducing growth rates in their first year in the sea. Fish already acclimatized to sea water before transfer begin feeding and growing much more quickly. Thirdly, having fish already acclimatized to sea water is an advantage for transportation by boat, which is commonly employed in Norway (see below).

TRANSPORT

It is usually necessary to transport salmon smolts or rainbow trout fingerlings from the relatively few units specializing in their production to the many fish farms specializing in growing-on the fish in the sea. Frequently journeys of hundreds of kilometres are necessary. The deeply indented nature of Norway's west coast, where most of the fish farms are situated, makes travel by land in a north-south direction difficult as one must frequently either drive many kilometres around fjords or use ferries to cross them. Except for delivery to inland farms, therefore, transport of fish by road tends to be limited to fairly short journeys. Most farms get their smolts or fingerlings delivered by sea.

Transport by road

Even when long distance transport is to be by sea it is necessary to get the young fish from their growing tanks to a wharf from where a ship can collect them, and this part of the journey has to be by road. Many smolt and fingerling units are located on the coast, but some are not and their fish may have some distance to travel to a harbour.

Containers for transporting fish by road are usually of fibreglass, made to travel on the back of a truck or on a trailer (*Fig* 32). For short distance transport a single skin is sufficient, but for longer journeys insulated tanks having walls of two layers of fibreglass with polyurethane foam between them are available to help keep the water inside cool. Commercially made tanks are available in a variety of sizes, commonly of 1,500–2,500 litres

Fig 32. A truck and trailer carrying fibreglass tanks containing live fish. (*Photograph: Norsk Landbrukskjemi A/S—Astra-Ewos A/B*).

capacity. In use they are filled to the top with water; part-filled tanks would be less stable and water slopping about could damage fish. Small fish can be carried in these tanks at densities up to $125\,kg/m^3$ of water, but $50–80\,kg/m^3$ is more commonly used. Larger fish could be carried in higher density as their oxygen demand is lower. Fish transported in fresh water can be carried at higher density than those in sea water due to the higher oxygen carrying capacity of the former. For long distance transport it is usual to carry fish in cold water, often around $5\,°C$, because the fish are less active and use less oxygen at low temperature. Approved anaesthetics can also be employed to keep fish quiet, but are not commonly used. Bottled oxygen can be carried and bubbled through the water from perforated pipes during the journey, or a pump can be used to mix air with the water. Fish should always be starved for two or three days before transport so that their digestive tracts are empty, otherwise they may vomit under handling, and this and their faeces would foul the water.

Smolts or fingerlings which leave their production units already acclimatized to sea water are of course transported in sea water, but those not previously acclimatized travel by road in fresh water. If the farms in which they are to be grown-on are reasonably close they go all the way by road, and on arrival are dumped directly into sea water cages with no

Fig 33. A tank for short-distance road transport of smolts, equipped with a fish pump.

61

apparent ill effects. But when fish are sold to'distant farms transport for most of the journey is usually by ship in sea water. To avoid subjecting them to the stresses of osmotic shock and transport simultaneously, which can cause losses, fish are sometimes first taken a short distance by road in fresh water to the nearest coast, where they are put into sea cages. They are then left for a few days to acclimatize to sea water before going aboard ships for the main part of their journey.

Before any journey begins the fish must be transferred from their growing tanks to the transport containers. This can be done with nets but, especially in the case of salmon smolts, which are very delicate and prone to mechanical damage, special suction pumps are often used to avoid handling the fish (*Fig* 33). The company A/S Mowi of Bergen has developed its own system to avoid handling smolts. At Mowi's biggest smolt unit, at Øyerhamn on the island of Varaldsøy in Hardangerfjord, the outlets from the smolt tanks all discharge into common raceways. These connect up to a wide flexible plastic pipe which ends just above the water surface of the fjord, where it is supported by a raft. When tank outlet screens are removed, fish and water flow by gravity out down the pipe, the end of which is first put directly into the hold of the transport vessel.

Fig 34. A live-hauling boat used to transport salmon smolts. (*Photograph: Vidar Vassvik*).

Fig 35. Smolts are poured from the road-transport tank into
the hold of a live-hauling boat through a flexible pipe.
(*Photograph: Vidar Vassvik*).

Smolts are therefore transported without any handling and without any
road transport being necessary.

Transport by sea

Transport of smolts and fingerlings by sea is one field in which Norway's
commercial fishing tradition has helped the new fish farming industry.
For many years it has been usual to transport live captured fish, notably
coalfish and cod, over long distances to market, and boats were developed

specially for this. The operators of these same boats now enjoy an extra income by contracting to collect young salmonids from the hatcheries and deliver them to the on-growing units.

A live-hauling boat externally resembles an inshore trawler in size and design (*Fig* 34). The difference is that the hold is made to be filled with water, creating a live-well in which fish are carried. Valves below water level on the sides of the boat towards the bow and stern can be opened so that water flows through the hold when the ship is under way. Mesh screens prevent escape of fish. When the boat is moored to load fish, diesel pumps circulate clean sea water through the hold. Smolt hatcheries are often located near an estuary so that they have access to both sea and fresh water. Boats may therefore have to anchor in water of low salinity while loading and, to prevent the fish being subjected to large fluctuations in salinity, it may be necessary to pump water up into the hold from deep in the sea. Hold valves can be closed while under way if the boat has to pass through an area of polluted water on its way to the customer's farm.

When direct transfer of smolts or fingerlings from growing tanks to the boat is not possible, and they must arrive by road, their road transport tanks can be swung aboard the boat with a power hoist before the fish are poured into the hold. Alternatively a long, flexible outlet pipe is attached to the tank and the fish run through this into the hold (*Fig* 35). Either way handling of fish is always kept to a minimum. The fibreglass tanks commonly used for road transport can, of course, be put aboard ordinary boats themselves for transport to fish farms.

Live-hauling boats can successfully transport smolts over thousands of kilometres if necessary, and long journeys take many days as speed must be kept low to avoid damage to fish. For short journeys fish can be transported in ordinary floating net cages, like those described in Chapter 7, towed behind a boat, but these can only travel very slowly. Floating fibreglass tanks through which water passes, and which are towed behind a boat, have also been used to transport smolts.

Transport by air

On occasions fish are transported by float-plane, either in special tanks or in plastic bags part filled with water and inflated with oxygen. Figures show that, under some circumstances, this method can be just as cheap as transport by road or sea.

64

5   Siting of Sea Units

Many of the quality requirements for fish farm water supplies discussed in Chapter 3 for fresh water also apply to sea water. Also there are special site requirements for different types of sea water fish farm, and some of these are considered in Chapters 6 and 7. Only those factors which are different in sea and fresh water, or are unique to the sea, and which are of relevance to most unit types, are considered in the present chapter.

TEMPERATURE AND ICE

Annual maximum and minimum temperatures recorded at stations all around the Norwegian coast were discussed in Chapter 1, and areas having the most suitable annual range of temperature for culture of salmonids were shown (*Fig* 2). However, within the area indicated there are many local variations in water temperature, especially in sheltered inshore areas. Such variations should be considered when selecting a precise site for a sea water fish farm.

Rainfall on the mountains of Norway's west coast is heavy, and large quantities of fresh water run off from the land, down rivers and streams, and out into the fjords. The fresh water entering the fjords in winter is very cold and because its density is lower than that of sea water it tends to float, forming a surface layer of low salinity. Because this is in close contact with the air, which has a temperature below zero for much of the winter, and it mixes only slowly with the warmer sea water underneath, it freezes. As a result the inner parts of many Norwegian fjords are frozen over for several months of the year. Fish can live in the warmer water under the ice, but the presence of ice would make it impossible to feed the fish artificially, and could cause serious damage to most types of unit construction. Fjords have other disadvantages as fish farm sites, notably poor water circulation, but ice is primarily the reason Norwegian fish farms are, contrary to popular misconception, generally not sited far inside fjords.

Even outside fjords there are areas through which currents habitually carry ice flows in winter, and fish units should obviously not be built in the path of these.

DEPTH AND SEA BOTTOM

Waste food and fish faeces fall from the bottom of floating net cage units onto the sea bed, where its decomposition uses oxygen. Plenty of clean, open water between the sea bed and the fish cages is therefore essential. A minimum depth of around 4–5m underneath cages should be maintained at all stages of the tide, and this means that cage units should not be sited in places with less than 8–10m depth at low water.

Even then, waste substances can build up on the bottom through successive years of unit operation to form a thick mud. There is a risk that this may come to a point where locally anaerobic conditions suddenly occur during a warm spell, with serious consequences for the fish. Such build-up of waste can also occur in enclosure-type units. Sites in which tidal currents are sufficiently strong to sweep away waste and prevent its build-up are therefore to be preferred, and preliminary examination of the sea bed at a potential site can give a good idea of its self-cleaning potential. A clean, rocky bottom with a wide variety of animal species, particularly lobsters, is a good sign.

WATER QUALITY

Oxygen

Sea water receives oxygen from three sources—by absorption from the air, by influx of oxygenated fresh water, and by photosynthesis of plants in the sea. The third process is the most important and, though rooted plants which produce oxygen by photosynthesis occur in shallow coastal areas, most of the oxygen is produced by microscopic plankton. Absorption from the air is less important in the sea than in fresh water, but is increased by wind and wave action.

The amount of oxygen that water will hold decreases with increasing salinity, so that sea water contains less oxygen than fresh water at the same temperature and pressure. However, clean water from the open sea is normally well oxygenated, though local shortages of oxygen can occur. Problems in fish farms are usually caused by the fishes' own oxygen demand and that of their decaying waste products and food, when water circulation is insufficient for the amount of stock held.

Pollution

Industrial pollution is slight around most of the Norwegian coast and a number of pollutants, *eg* heavy metals, are of less consequence to fish in the sea than in fresh water due to the chemical buffering capacity of the former.

Fouling of fish-retaining screens or nets, and of pipes and tanks, by growths of sessile marine organisms can be a serious problem, since it obstructs the flow of water through the fish enclosure. The stresses imposed by tidal currents on fish enclosures are also greater if these are fouled. It is essential, therefore, to clean screens and nets regularly, and to apply anti-fouling paints to reduce growth of the fouling organisms.

CURRENTS AND TIDES

It can be seen from the above paragraphs that a knowledge of the local water currents is of paramount importance when choosing a site for a salt water fish farm, and that water quality problems in sea units usually only occur when currents are inadequate.

Currents serve two functions: to supply clean, oxygen-rich water to the fish, and to remove their metabolic products, faeces and waste food.

At most sites the strongest currents are provided by the tide, and therefore flow in two opposite directions as the tide rises and falls. To get the best possible water exchange, the unit should be orientated with its longest side at right angles to the current.

At the extreme southern tip of Norway is a 'neutral zone' where there is no tidal rise and fall, and close to this area tidal currents are absent or slight. The difference between the level of high and low tide increases as one goes further north along the coast until, in the extreme north of the country, it is about 3.5m on spring tides. In some areas the tidal currents can be too strong and put too much stress on unit structures. According to Braaten and Sætre (1973) peak tidal flows of between 10 and 50 centimetres per second are ideal for most types of unit using fish netting enclosures or floating cages. However, considerably lower flow rates than this are satisfactory. Formulae for calculating the stresses imposed by tidal currents on fish farm structures have been given by Milne (1972).

Some information on tidal currents along the Norwegian coast is available in a government publication called the *Norwegian pilot,* but sufficiently accurate local information can be hard to obtain. A prospective fish farmer can, however, measure currents himself using drogues which can be adjusted to move with the current at any depth required.

SHELTER

Apart from favourable water temperature, the greatest advantage of the Norwegian coast for siting fish farms is an abundance of sheltered sites. The most favoured areas for most types of unit are channels between islands or between an island and the mainland, where there is also a good flow of water provided by tides or currents.

Any farm construction which stands above water level for all or part of the tidal cycle, or is built on-shore, is subject to wind action and must be designed to withstand the maximum gust speeds occurring in the vicinity. Data on wind speed and direction are collected routinely by a series of government weather observation stations all along the coast, and are published each year in the *Norwegian Meteorological Yearbook.* This also gives information on sea water temperatures. The Norwegian Meteorological Institute has also issued a publication giving measurements for the period 1931–1960, and the expected long-term extremes of wind speed for an area can be obtained from these.

Underwater parts of fish farm constructions, and floating cages, must also withstand wave forces. The highest wave to be expected in an area can be calculated from the direction and speed of wind, the fetch length, *ie* the distance of open water between the unit and the nearest land in the direction from which the wind blows, and the water depth variations along the fetch. A method for calculating wave heights and forces from these parameters is given by Milne (1972).

LEGAL FACTORS AND ACCESS

Ownership

Most land in Norway is privately owned and, according to law, this ownership extends to the foreshore and out into the sea to the depth in which a horse can stand. The public is, however, allowed access over private land. Most of the land is owned in small pieces by the families who live on them, and whose ancestors have done so for generations. There is no real 'aristocracy' owning large areas populated by tenants. The majority of fish farms in Norway are small, and have been started by the owners of the adjacent land themselves. Larger companies which have started production requiring the use of bigger areas of land have often had to lease this from many owners, some of whom they also employ.

Licencing

Even if a man owns the land he must obtain a licence from the Department of Fisheries before he can start farming fish. To obtain this he must submit a detailed plan giving the number and size of proposed units, their proposed location, amount of fish to be produced, *etc*. After the licence is granted his farm must be ready for inspection at any time, and he can be forced to modify or close the unit if it is unsatisfactory on grounds of disease or hygiene, or causes an obstruction to navigation. Units must also be 'appropriately marked', including with lights at night, so that they are easily visible to shipping.

Access

When selecting a coastal site for a fish farm, requirements for all services and for accessibility are much the same as outlined for fresh water units in Chapter 3. However, sea units require much larger amounts of foodstuffs, not only because they produce larger fish but also because 50% of farms still use 'wet' foods which are much bulkier to transport than dry foods and which cannot be stored as easily. It is therefore even more important for a sea unit to be sited close to a harbour or other source of food, which is frequently delivered by sea.

Supervision

Sea units hold considerable quantities of very valuable fish right up to marketable size, so supervision to prevent theft of stock is even more important than for the majority of fresh water units, which produce small fish only. If the owner or manager does not live within sight of his unit thefts can be expected. Small-scale thefts may not be important, provided the thief does not damage the enclosure and allow the rest of the stock to escape. However, occasions have arisen, *eg* on the island of Hitra (an area of much fish farming activity), where floating nets have been emptied by thieves, presumably operating as an organized gang with transport and markets for tonnes of fish duly arranged beforehand.

F

6 Fixed Sea Units

SEA ENCLOSURES

Sea enclosures are here defined as impoundments of sea water in which most of the circumference is formed by the natural shore-line. Man-made barriers, which permit the passage of water, complete the enclosure.

Several enclosures of this type have been built in Norway, but the only really important ones still in operation are those of the company A/S Mowi. Mowi is the largest producer of farmed salmon in Norway, and at present in the world. It produces about 500 tonnes of fish each year in two sea enclosures of unique design, situated between islands in the vicinity of Møvik, near Bergen.

Construction of A/S Mowi's enclosures

Veløykjølpo. At Veløykjølpo, the largest of Mowi's enclosures, 3.5ha of water between the islands of Sotra and Veløy is fenced off by concrete dams placed at each end of the natural channel (*Fig* 36). The dams (*Fig* 37) hold screens consisting of vertical aluminium bars with 11 mm gaps between them. Screens are located in the concrete by moulded guideways and are removable. Each screen position has two guideways, one behind the other, so that when a screen is removed for cleaning a replacement can first be put in the duplicate guideway to prevent fish escaping. Screens are removed by a gantry which travels on wheels along the top of the dam.

Building at Veløykjølpo was completed in 1970. The original intention was to allow the 1.5 m tide and natural currents to effect water exchange, but it soon became apparent that water flowing out of the enclosure on the ebb tide frequently returned on the next flood. A further problem was that circulation in the deepest parts of the enclosure was insufficient to prevent the build-up of organic matter from waste food and fish faeces. The danger

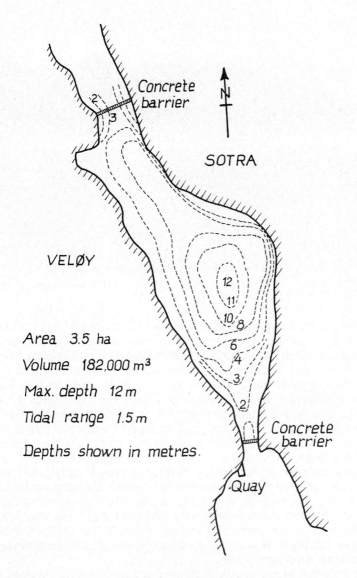

Concrete
barrier

SOTRA

VELØY

12
11
10 8
6
4
3
2

Area 3.5 ha

Volume 182,000 m³

Max. depth 12 m

Tidal range 1.5 m

Depths shown in metres.

Concrete
barrier

Quay

Fig 36. Plan of A/S Mowi's sea enclosure at Veløykjølpo. (*From Milne, 1972*).

71

Fig 37. The concrete barrier at the south end of A/S Mowi's sea enclosure at Veløyk-jølpo. (*Photograph: Lars Bull-Berg*).

of de-oxygenation in parts of the enclosure therefore severely limited the crop of fish maintainable there. Mowi has solved this problem by installing electrically driven pumps which suck water and sludge from the deepest areas and discharge it just outside the south dam. Overlapping rubber flaps outside the aluminium screens of the dam act as valves to prevent discharged water flowing back into the enclosure. All flow through the enclosure is therefore one way, from north to south. Normally two pumps, each moving about 120,000 litres of water per minute, are in operation, and their suction ends are screened to prevent them taking in fish. Additional through-flow is created by large electrically driven propellers mounted on floats. One of these is permanently positioned to blow water out through the south dam and another circulates water round the enclosure. The high density of fish now held in Veløykjølpo is entirely dependent on these pumps to obtain sufficient clean sea water. Mowi estimates that, in the event of a power failure, it has only a few hours before the fish begin to die. A large diesel generator is therefore essential as a back-up supply of power.

Flogøykjølpo. Mowi's second, smaller sea enclosure at Flogøykjølpo was completed in 1969. It has an area of about 1.2 ha and maximum water depth of 10 m (*Fig* 38). Screens used are of vertical steel bars spaced 15 mm apart. They are not removable for cleaning so this must be

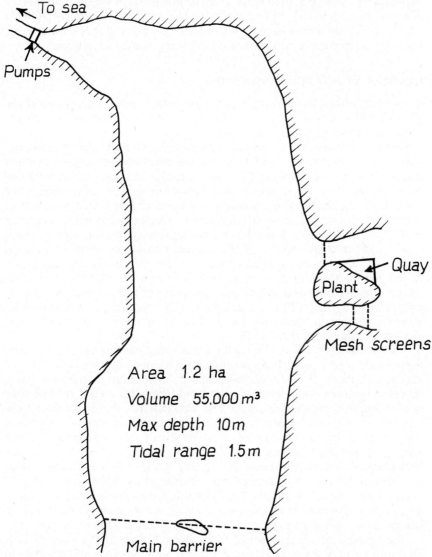

Fig 38. Plan of A/S Mowi's sea enclosure at Flogøykjølpo. (*Modified from Milne, 1972*).

done by divers. A main barrier spans the south end of the enclosure, with two subsidiary screens on the east side. Four new pumps, each of 2.5 m³/sec capacity, were installed in 1973 at the north end of the enclosure and a channel through to the sea was made. As at Veløykjølpo, flow through the enclosure is one way, this time south to north, and the side channels are now considered unimportant for maintaining water circulation.

Operation of A/S Mowi's enclosures

Growth of salmon in sea water from smolt to final harvest takes two years. Mowi obtains annual production by harvesting and stocking at Veløykjølpo and Flogøykjølpo in alternate years.

Oxygenation and stock control. The standing crop of salmon maintainable in the enclosures is limited by the balance between oxygen demand and the flow rate of sea water through the enclosures, which is determined by pump capacity. Mowi regularly measures oxygen concentration in the water entering and leaving each enclosure and also in the deeper parts of enclosures. Incoming water is sometimes supersaturated with oxygen up to 115%, and outgoing water has an average concentration 2 ppm lower.

The oxygen consumption of the salmon, considered together with the water temperature and known capacity of the pumps, is one indication Mowi has of the standing crop of fish present at any time. Further indications are obtained by periodic sampling of fish by seine netting, to estimate average size. This is multiplied by the number of smolts stocked, minus a percentage figure for losses. Losses between smolt and harvest are, on average, less than 15%.

The standing crop of fish which each enclosure can comfortably support all year round, maintaining oxygen concentration at 6 ppm or above, is known. For Veløykjølpo about 280 tonnes is the safe limit, though in winter considerably more could be held. Every second year nearly 300,000 smolts are stocked in Veløykjølpo. After one year their average weight will be nearly 1 kg, and after two years may approach 4 kg. With losses so low, continuous harvesting is necessary after the first year to keep the standing crop down to the safe level. Continuous harvesting also means a much higher total crop of fish is obtained than would be if Mowi only stocked the number of smolts which could be allowed to grow for two years. Veløykjølpo, for example, produces about 600 tonnes of salmon in its two-year cycle. Processing and marketing also benefit from having fish slaughtered regularly rather than all at one time.

The amount of water pumped through enclosures is the same at Flogøykjølpo and Veløykjølpo, so in theory both units should be able to produce the same amount of salmon. In practice fish grow less well at the smaller unit, where the two-yearly production is only 400 tonnes. This disparity between productions in alternate years is a problem to Mowi as costs tend to be constant rather than proportional to production and markets demand an even supply. The company is therefore thinking of building a third enclosure to run in phase with Flogøykjølpo. Several possible sites have been surveyed. An alternative would be to increase the pumping capacity at Flogøykjølpo, and in fact there is scope for increasing production from both units by this method.

Harvest. All salmon remaining in a sea enclosure two years after stocking are harvested. A four-sided trap net is used repeatedly to catch fish. One side is lowered, a water current created by a propeller machine lures fish in, and the lowered side is then raised. Fish are removed from the trap with power-lifted dip nets (*Fig* 39). When the trap catch becomes low, remaining fish are captured in gill nets. As a last resort Mowi uses explosives to kill elusive salmon, as none must be left to feed on the next stock of smolts.

As soon as Mowi is satisfied that all large salmon have been removed, the enclosure is re-stocked with smolts to begin its next two-year cycle.

Fig 39. Removing salmon from a trap net in one of A/S Mowi's sea enclosures. (*Photograph: Lars Bull-Berg*).

75

Site requirements

Unfortunately, some of the site requirements for sea enclosures are contradictory. The intention when all Norway's sea enclosures were built was to allow natural tides and currents to effect water exchange. Sites through which strong natural currents flowed were therefore essential. A/S Mowi's Veløykjølpo site, through which excellent natural currents flow from end to end, is an apparently perfect example. However, so that the solid barriers necessary to contain the fish can be built at reasonable cost, fairly shallow areas of water with a firm bottom are needed at the ends of enclosures. Hence sea enclosures tend to be shallow at each end and deep in the middle and natural currents, no matter how strong, tend to change only the surface layers of water, passing over the deeper layers which they leave relatively undisturbed. With the high intensity of feeding and high fish stocking density necessary to make the enclosures an economic proposition, a build-up of waste food and fish faeces in the deeper parts of enclosures, leading to the danger of de-oxygenation, is inevitable.

By pumping, Mowi has solved this problem well but only at high cost. Disregarding the capital costs of pumps and emergency generators, Mowi estimates that the electric power required for pumping alone adds 30–40 øre (100 øre = 1 Norwegian krone) to the cost of each kilo of salmon produced. For smaller farmers who started production in sea enclosures the costs of pumping equipment on the Mowi scale were prohibitive. Some of these workers have therefore abandoned this system in favour of floating cages. The few who stayed with sea enclosures have had no alternative but to keep their stocking rates very much lower than they originally intended.

Evaluation of sea enclosures

The main disadvantages of Mowi-type enclosures are the high capital costs of building the barriers and of pumping equipment, and the running costs of pumps. Once the initial investment has been made, the system has several important advantages over the more commonly used cage culture method (Chapter 7). Mowi's enclosures, for example, have considerably longer working lives than cages and are much less prone to loss of fish through storm damage. Using Mowi's special feeding system (Chapter 8) labour costs for feeding a given number of fish are less than in floating cages.

Mowi's stock control is very good. It is often said that the farmer has better access to his fish in floating cages than in sea enclosures, and certainly harvest is easier. However, the feasibility of, for example, removing all fish from net cages for disease treatment by bathing or individual dosing is highly questionable when one is dealing with the quantities of fish Mowi produces, which would require the use of over 100 large cages.

ON-SHORE ENCLOSURES

In the early days of salt water salmonid farming in Norway several units using fixed on-shore enclosures were built. These units consist basically of concrete ponds or raceways sited adjacent to the sea just above high-tide level. Clean sea water has to be pumped up to the ponds and this is expensive. Consequently most of the units originally set up to produce large rainbow trout or, less commonly, salmon have either closed down or changed over to producing smolts and fingerlings to be grown-on in floating net cages. Fixed on-shore enclosures are therefore now mainly of historical interest.

Design of unit

One concrete pond unit which has been adapted to keep pace with modern techniques is that belonging to Mr Magne Gjerstad at Hjelset, near Molde. Situated on the Fannefjord, the farm consists of seven rectangular concrete ponds bordered on one side by the fjord and on the landward side by a hatchery building and dwelling (*Fig* 40). The ponds are constructed of poured reinforced concrete and are arranged in two rows. Closest to the sea is a row of three large ponds, each 13 m × 14 m in area and with 2 m depth of water. Parallel to these on their on-shore side is a row of four smaller tanks, each 10 m × 8 m with 1 m depth of water.

Each larger pond is of the circulating type. Water enters tangentially and leaves by a central screened drain to which the tank bottom slopes. The drain is connected by a wide pipe under the pond bottom to an external concrete 'monk' on the downhill side of the pond immediately adjacent to the sea shore. Water level in the pond is determined by the number of wooden boards inserted in the monk, in the same way as is commonly used in many countries with earth ponds. With all boards removed the pond empties itself for cleaning. The smaller ponds work on the same principle as the large ones, but they discharge into an open concrete channel between the two rows of ponds instead of directly into the sea. All ponds are regularly painted with anti-foulant.

Sea water is pumped from the fjord by three large electric pumps, and a back-up diesel generator is available in the event of power failure. Water

Fig 40. Concrete ponds for rainbow trout culture in sea water.

enters a concrete head tank situated under the pumping shed, from where it flows out along the channel between the two rows of ponds. From here it flows by gravity down into the large ponds, but has to be pumped again by a smaller submersible electric pump up to another concrete channel on the upstream side of the small ponds. It then flows into these by gravity. The smaller ponds also receive fresh water by gravity from the hatchery.

Operation of the unit

Mr Gjerstad's unit started production of large rainbow trout about 1963. Fingerlings produced in the hatchery were transferred to the smaller concrete ponds in spring and acclimatized gradually to sea water through several intermediate salinities. When the larger ponds were emptied in autumn, the new fish were graded out into them and grown until the following autumn. By harvest time each large pond contained about seven tonnes of fish, *ie* about $20 \, \text{kg/m}^3$.

In 1970 the unit stopped producing table trout in this way. The concrete ponds are now used only for producing rainbow trout fingerlings and salmon smolts. These are subsequently transferred to floating net cages, of which Mr Gjerstad has 20. The large ponds now each produce about five tonnes of small fish per year. The unit's total annual production is 15 tonnes of rainbow trout fingerlings and 60,000 salmon smolts. Of these, 10 tonnes of the trout and 50,000 of the smolts are sold to other

78

farms. Mr Gjerstad's own 20 cages produce around 60 tonnes of trout and salmon each year. The entire production cycle of hatchery, ponds and floating cages is run by three men.

Evaluation of on-shore units

The high costs of pumping sea water make fixed on-shore units uncompetitive with floating cage production of food fish. Mr Gjerstad, for example, estimates that pumping water to his concrete ponds costs about NKr 30,000 per year for electricity, whereas water exchange to his floating nets is of course provided free by natural tides and currents. Building costs for concrete structures are also very high. Consequently no-one today would start up a new unit of this type except to produce fingerlings and smolts, which must be cultured in on-shore facilities (Chapter 4). Nevertheless at present a few older farms do still produce food fish in on-shore tanks or raceways. This is feasible while prices of fish are so high (Chapter 10), but if profit margins get slimmer in the future these units might be expected to become uneconomic before those of other types.

NETTING ENCLOSURES

Fixed enclosures of a unique type have been successfully operated at Bjordal on Fuglesettfjord, an arm of Sognefjord, by Mr Erling Osland since 1963. The enclosures are formed on one side by the natural beach, and on the other three by a wall of nylon fish netting hung from poles driven into the sea bed (*Fig* 41).

Construction of enclosures

Mr Osland operates nine netting enclosures, each of about 700 m² area and 4 m water depth at low tide. At each side of an enclosure, where it joins the beach, concrete walls about 3 m long have been built to provide a solid footing for the net. Around the rest of the perimeter of each enclosure heavy posts of impregnated timber are embedded at 5 m intervals 3 m down into the sea bed, and extend for about 2 m out of the water at the highest tide (*Fig* 42). Cross pieces of timber near the tops of the poles form T-structures, the horizontal arms of which are drilled to hold ropes which support the netting barrier itself. Originally a double barrier was used, one layer of netting suspended from the inside arm and one from the outside. The outside barrier was intended to exclude floating debris and to ensure against escape of fish if the inside barrier became

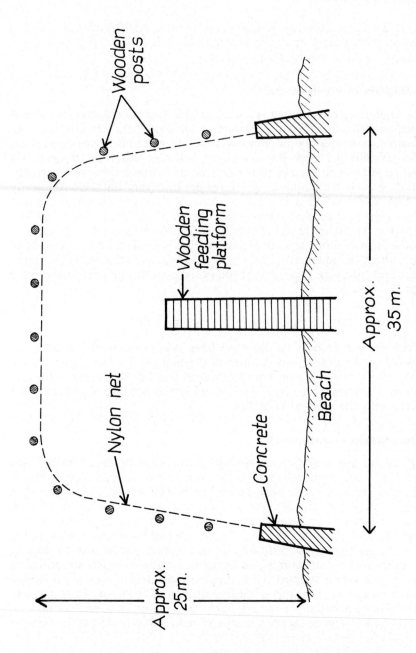

Fig 41. Diagram of a nylon netting sea enclosure.

holed. However, the outside barrier was found unnecessary and its presence tended to restrict water flow through the enclosure. Nowadays only a single layer of netting is used, suspended on the inside of the poles (*Fig* 43). At the bottom of the poles, under water, the net barrier is fixed by a rope running through galvanized eyes. The net then turns inwards and runs along the sea bed for about 1 m, until it terminates in a lead line. The net, normally of knotless netting, tends to embed itself in the sand on the sea bottom, forming a perfect seal, and extends up for at least 1 m out of the water at the highest tide to prevent fish jumping out.

A wooden platform, from which wet food is thrown to the fish by hand from a wheelbarrow, extends out over the water to the middle of each enclosure.

Operation of netting enclosures

Management of netting enclosures is in many ways similar to that of floating net cages (Chapter 7). Mr Osland has his own hatchery and freshwater pond system to produce rainbow trout fingerlings and salmon smolts. At present his food fish production is mostly of rainbow trout. Salmon represent only 20–30%. Both fingerlings and smolts are stocked out in spring, *ie* May–June. Only one enclosure is needed for salmon in their first year in the sea, but young rainbow trout normally occupy at

Fig 42. One of Mr Osland's netting enclosures.

81

least two enclosures. Rainbow trout are grown for 18 months and salmon for 2 years, and after 6–12 months the fish are graded out into new enclosures as they become empty following harvest. Nets must be changed at intervals, cleaned and re-impregnated with anti-foulant (Chapter 7). Mr Osland finds it necessary to do this only once a year, so he is seldom obliged to change a net around an enclosure which still has fish in it. If this does have to be done, however, a second net can be hung on the outside of the posts to prevent escape of fish. Nets of larger mesh size are used for fish in their second year in the sea.

Fish are harvested by repeatedly seining an enclosure. If one or two fish evade capture they will escape to sea when the net is removed for cleaning, and will therefore not present a predator problem to the new young fish. Each enclosure can comfortably hold about 20 tonnes of harvest-ready

Fig 43. The net barrier of an "Osland" enclosure.

82

fish, and Mr Osland's sea water production approaches 100 tonnes of trout and salmon per year with a staff of four. In addition to the salmonids, a useful side-crop of flatfish is obtained. Many small flounder and plaice are attracted by the prospect of free food into the enclosures when they are small enough to pass through the meshes of the net. Once there they grow well and are soon too big to get out again. Several tonnes of such wild fish can be harvested each year, and Mr Osland is collaborating with the Norwegian Institute of Marine Research in experiments in which young flatfish are deliberately stocked into his enclosures as a second crop.

In the event that the dissolved oxygen level in an enclosure falls to dangerously low levels at slack tide during the summer, a floating electric propeller machine capable of circulating 20,000 litres of water per minute is available. In practice it is very rarely necessary to use this.

Evaluation of netting enclosures

As Mr Osland's unit is clearly successful one might wonder why a similar system has not been adopted elsewhere in Norway. The reason is probably that the site on Fuglesettfjord is rather special. Enclosures of this type present a large area of netting to the wind when the tide is low, and are therefore much more prone to storm damage than floating cages which rise and fall with the tide. Mr Osland's site is exceptionally well sheltered. Water currents close to the shore are also apparently perfect, being strong enough to remove wastes and prevent the build-up of mud on the bottom of enclosures, but not so strong that they put excessive strain on the netting or fish. The water is also free of debris and ice which could hole enclosures. Fouling of the netting seems to be slower than that encountered at most sites around the Norwegian coast, where it is necessary to change the net bags of floating cages at least twice a year (Chapter 7). However, most fouling occurs in the top two metres of water and, in Osland-type enclosures, this area is continually cleaned by exposure to the air as the tide rises and falls.

Mr Osland's enclosures have a much shorter working life than Mowi-type enclosures or on-shore raceways, but probably longer than floating net cages. It is estimated that the posts supporting the nets will last about 20 years, and the nets themselves about five years. Netting enclosures would cost more to build than net cages but, as feeding is done from the land without the use of a boat, in everyday use net enclosures are really more comparable to cages equipped with a floating walkway from the shore (Chapter 7). The costs of netting enclosures and cages thus equipped are probably not so different. In common with other enclosure systems, harvest is more difficult than from floating cages.

7 Floating Net Cages

Floating net cages have been used for many years by fishermen along Norway's coast for storing captured fish alive. Before the days of deep-freezing it was extremely useful to be able to hold live fish until a convenient time for transport to market. A number of species, especially coalfish and cod, were kept in water right up to arrival at the markets in the special live-hauling boats described in Chapter 4. Floating net cages were also used to store small fishes for future use as bait for the long-line fishery. It was a logical extension of this storage function to feed and grow small fish until they reached harvestable size in captivity in floating cages, though this has so far proved economic only for salmonids.

The use of floating cages is now by far the most popular method in Norway for growing-on small rainbow trout or salmon smolts up to harvestable size. Though a few small units operate in lakes, the vast majority are in sea water.

CAGE DESIGN

General construction

Floating net cages used for salmonid culture in Norway are usually of simple design. Basically, they consist of a fish-net bag which is open at the top, where it is suspended from a floating framework. The bag hangs loose in the sea, but is kept roughly in shape by stones or other sinkers tied in small net pockets in the bottom corners, frequently 2–3 kg for each corner. Nets are usually 4–6 m deep. The net is either extended, or an extra net is attached, up out of the water for about a metre all round the top of the bag to prevent fish jumping out. When small fish are present in the cage, a further net of larger mesh size covers the open top of the bag to exclude predatory birds.

84

Most fish farmers buy ready-made net bags, but many construct their own floating framework. Most model these on a few designs which have been successfully used since the early days of sea water salmonid culture. However, commercially produced cages are now available and are gaining wide acceptance. Size of cage can be anything up to $1000\,m^3$, but is normally between 100 and $500\,m^3$.

The simplest unit to make holds a net of four vertical sides and of rectangular cross-section, but most fish farmers prefer nets approximating to circular cross-section. This is partly because round nets give the best volume/area ratio, but also because many people feel that round nets are more suited to the fishes' observed habit of swimming in circles in the cage. Since the basic building material for the home-made framework of cages is timber, it is not easy to make a truly circular structure, but approximations to it are made by using six, eight or even ten sides. The six-sided cages used by the Vik brothers at Sykkylven have been widely imitated, but more popular still is an eight-sided structure as used by the Grøntvedt brothers at Hitra. This holds a net bag of $500\,m^3$.

'Grøntvedt'-type cage

The floating framework for a Grøntvedt-type cage consists of eight sides, each 5 m long. These are constructed separately both for convenience in transport and so that they can be linked together by more or less flexible joints to reduce rigidity of the structure and allow some movement in the sea. Each side-section is usually constructed of timber, which must be impregnated to reduce rotting. Planks of $5'' \times 2''$ ($= 12.7 \times 5.1\,cm$, but timber is still measured in inches in Norway) or larger form the sides of the section, and are spaced 30 cm apart by wooden slats nailed across the top and bottom. At the top the slats should be close enough together to be walked on comfortably because in the finished structure the tops of the frame sections provide a catwalk all the way around the net. Between the two layers of slats the flotation substance, usually expanded polystyrene, is sandwiched. In Norway expanded polystyrene is frequently sold in blocks $1\,m \times 2\,m \times 30\,cm$, and this is one reason for the 30 cm width often used for frame sections. Strips of $2\,m \times 30\,cm \times$ the required depth (often $5''$) are easily cut from these blocks and two strips fit comfortably end to end inside each section. They are held in place by nails driven through the timber from above and below.

The joint between each two neighbouring sections of the frame is often formed by bolting strips of old car tyres, or heavy rubberized machine belts, over the inside and outside of the join. As a safety precaution in case this breaks, either a heavy nylon rope or a hollow flexible plastic pipe

85

containing a cable extends right around the outside of all eight sections, to each of which it is securely fastened. At every second corner, (*ie* in four corners) a loop of rope inside flexible plastic pipe is fixed through holes bored in the wood to provide anchoring points for the whole structure (*Fig* 44).

Traditionally, the net bag which holds the fish hangs down from the outside of the Grøntvedt-type floating framework. It is fixed securely to the top outer edge of each section by strips of 2″ × 2″ timber which hold the net between themselves and the underlying timber frame to which they are nailed. The rope or plastic pipe extending all the way round the outside of the structure holds the net off the framework thus preventing abrasion to the net.

Timber posts are nailed vertically onto the inside of the floating frame sections, and extend up for about one metre to hold a strip of net which prevents fish jumping out. However, having the net bag fixed to the outside of the framework makes handling of the net during net changing, fish harvesting *etc* more difficult, and many workers now fix the net on the inside instead. This eliminates the need for a separate net as an 'anti-jumping' fence because the net bag can simply be pulled up a metre out of the water. The net bag can be fixed to the floats using wooden battens as

Fig 44. A Grøntvedt-type floating net cage.

86

described above, or hung on hooks attached to the timber.

Refinements of the Grøntvedt frame are commercially available. For example, the company SIAS Catamaran at Surnadal produces sealed glassfibre floats filled with expanded polystyrene, which are joined together by special galvanized hinges. The unit is marketed complete with net bag and anchoring fittings. Glassfibre covered floats are better than bare polystyrene not only because they provide much more structural strength, but also because uncovered polystyrene eventually becomes waterlogged and loses buoyancy. Truly circular floating frames are also available in sealed fibreglass, sections being linked by hinges. The moulded sections come complete with galvanized ferrules for attaching vertical posts for anti-jump fences, moulded holes to take hooks which hold the net bag, and attachment points for anchoring. Such circular units are manufactured by EBO, Orkanger.

Many home-made modifications of the Grøntvedt-type cage are in use. Frequently the flotation substance is fixed underneath the timber frame instead of sandwiched within it, and sections of the frame are solidly bolted together at the corners.

It is thought by some fish farmers that salmon require more room to swim about than rainbow trout, and some larger cages have been tried. Mr Oscar Torrissen, for example, who runs a large and successful farm in the north of Norway near Bodø, has tried making oval shaped cages by extending the Grøntvedt unit with two extra side pieces (*Fig* 45). Unfortunately the larger net required for this cage has proved much more difficult to handle, and Mr Torrissen is returning to conventional units.

Four and six-sided cages

Frames for six-sided cages can be of the same construction as Grøntvedt units but, especially with smaller cages, many farmers have constructed very simple, cheap units which are nonetheless successful in operation. Often frames are composed of a single layer of slats on a frame, rather than the double layer described. The ends of adjacent sides simply overlap and are joined directly by bolts. This forms a solid framework, but apparently the flexibility of the timber itself allows sufficient movement to accommodate sea-swell. Flotation is by expanded polystyrene blocks held in place under the slats by strips of galvanized metal which encircle the floats and are nailed at each side to the timber. A variety of home-made square cages is also in use in Norwegian fish farms. There is in fact no limit to the possible variation in design of home-made cage flotation frames, and the individual farmer's ingenuity can result in a good, cheap system to suit his own preferences.

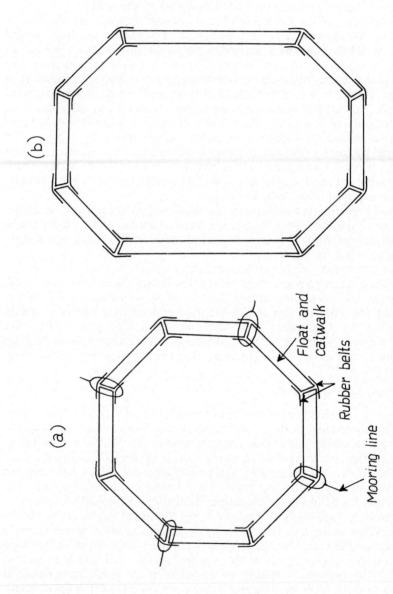

(a)

(b)

Mooring line

Rubber belts

Float and catwalk

Fig 45. Arrangement of flotation units in (a) a conventional Grøntvedt-type cage, (b) an experimental oval-shaped modification of a Grøntvedt cage.

'Tess' cage

In 1973, the company T Skretting A/S of Stavanger introduced to the market a new type of floating cage which it sells as a complete unit including net bag. This unit, called the 'Tess 300', has since gained wide acceptance in Norway, as well as being the best selling Norwegian-made cage for export. The system was actually designed by an employee of Egersund Trawlverksted, the company which manufactures the net bags for the unit, which are normally 4.5 m deep and 300 m³ capacity.

Flotation for the six-sided net is provided by six inflatable rubber buoys, each of 180 cm circumference, one at each corner of the net. The buoys are kept spread by six hollow fibreglass poles, each 7 m long, of 43 mm outside and 38 mm inside diameter. One end of each of these poles passes through a buoy, whilst the other screws into a common galvanized steel plate 3–4 m in the air above the centre of the net. The poles therefore resemble the spokes of an open umbrella (*Fig 46*). A rope sewn into the net bag one metre from the top all the way round is fastened to metal eyes on sleeves around the poles just above the floats. This rope, and hence the net, is kept taut by the outward pressure of the poles and buoys. The top edge of the net itself is tied to each pole 1 m higher to form the anti-jump fence.

Fig 46. The "Tess 300" cage, marketed by T Skretting A/S. (*Photograph: Arne Kittelsen*).

'Sterner' cage

The same company now also sells a new system invented by a Swede, Mr Tore Sterner. Sterner cages come in three sizes: 50, 100 and $200\,m^3$, and are of square cross-section. Flotation is provided by four, six, or eight inflatable rubber buoys (according to size of cage) each of 160 cm circumference. Each buoy supports a short length of octagonal aluminium tube vertically above it, and through holes in these the main horizontal supporting tubes pass, about 1 m above the water surface. These tubes are also of aluminium, but of circular cross-section, and are held in place in the vertical corner tubes of the unit with screw-tight aluminium collars. The top edge of the net bag has a sewn-in rope all around it, and at the corners loops of this rope pass around the vertical aluminium tubes to stretch the net taut. The rope is also fixed at intervals along the horizontal tubes with special rubber clips, and as these tubes are well above the water surface there is no need for any further height of net to prevent fish jumping out. However, anti-predator nets are easily fitted over the top of the structure, also stretched by ropes between vertical corner tubes. These cage units can be completed by the addition of Sterner battery-operated automatic dry food dispensers as described in Chapter 8. These are supported on further horizontal aluminium tubes fixed across the centre of the net (*Fig* 47).

Fig 47. A Sterner floating cage with an independent battery driven automatic feeder. (*Photograph: T Skretting A/S*).

90

Comparison of different cage types

Floating cage culture is such a new thing in Europe that there is as yet little scientific evidence as to what characteristics are desirable in cage design. Grøntvedt and similar cage types have stood the test of time and proved reliable in all weather conditions over the past 15 years. As their framework is made of timber they can be home-made, which keeps their price low, and they can easily be modified according to the farmer's own ideas. In use, the Grøntvedt cage's biggest advantage is that the wooden slats on top of the floats (or the sealed fibreglass floats themselves) provide a catwalk all around the net which is useful to stand on when feeding and harvesting fish or changing the net. The Skretting and Sterner cages do not have this feature. Consequently, except in fish farms which have their nets moored alongside a floating walkway, all work on cages must be done by boat, or they must be towed in to a quay. Both these cages are, however, quick and easy to assemble. The Skretting unit has proved reliable in the four years for which it has been used, and the materials in this and the Sterner cage are likely to outlast timber. The Sterner cage has not been in operation long, but it appears that some wear occurs at the corners of the frame where the horizontal and vertical aluminium tubes join. The design will shortly be modified to overcome this, probably by sheathing the ends of the horizontals with nylon. If this problem is solved, the Sterner unit with its special feeders will provide a useful cage system at a reasonable cost.

Truly circular cages are under test in several farms. Their frames are constructed from flexible plastic water-pipe with the ends welded together (*Fig* 48). Such cages are expensive but if experiments show that fish growth or survival is improved their use can be expected to increase. However, if no difference is found, the use of rectangular cages will probably increase because of their relative cheapness and simplicity of construction.

Net bags and fouling

Construction of nets. In Norway, the net bags which actually enclose the fish in floating cage systems are always made of nylon fish netting. Experiments in other countries, *eg* Scotland (Milne, 1972) have shown that other materials, especially galvanized weldmesh, are much more resistant to marine fouling. However, Norwegian fish farmers feel that the vastly greater cost of these materials, together with the extra difficulties involved in handling the more rigid nets during harvest, would make them uneconomic for use in local units.

91

The nylon netting used is strong (frequently gauge no. $4\frac{1}{2}$–8), and of a stretched mesh size varying usually from 10 mm for very small fish up to a 'standard' size of 15 mm, though for large fish considerably bigger mesh size can be used. Most fish farmers use knotted netting because it is less prone to tearing than the knotless type. Several Norwegian fishing net manufacturers produce standard-sized net bags, and they will also make up a special size or design to fill an individual farmer's requirements. It is rarely worth a farmer's trouble to make his own.

Fouling. Nets become fouled with marine growth of all sorts: weed, bivalve molluscs, crustaceans, sponges *etc.* Fouling tends to block the holes in the net, and thus restrict the movement of water through the cage. The volume of water within the net bag cannot, of course, carry enough oxygen to support the high density of fish stocked in it, and the fish are dependent on efficient exchange of water between the inside and outside of their cage both to bring in oxygen and remove their waste products. Nets must therefore be removed and replaced by clean ones before meshes become too obstructed by fouling organisms. Though the rate at which fouling builds up on nets varies from place to place, it is usually necessary to change nets twice per year. As fouling is seasonal, growing faster in warmer weather, nets are generally changed once in spring and again in late summer.

To change a net, first the sides of the net are pulled part-way up and hung on the cage framework (*Fig* 49). The fastenings around the top of the net are sufficiently loosened to allow the new net to be slipped underneath it and fastened to the frame so that it completely surrounds the old net. The remaining fastenings of the old net are then removed, one side is dropped into the water inside the new net, and the old net is pulled up from the other side. The fish gradually swim over into the new net without being handled. When dirty nets are removed for cleaning, new ones of larger mesh size can be substituted as the fish in the cage grow bigger. A net bag properly looked after will last a number of years, but should be tested regularly if used for more than about three years.

Fouled nets can be cleaned straight away with a high-pressure water jet, but the fouling organisms come off more easily if the net is first hung up to dry or kept in a light-proof container for a few days to kill them. New nets are bought ready impregnated with an anti-fouling preparation which slows down the rate of colonization of the net by marine organisms. If this substance is not periodically renewed throughout the life of the net, more frequent cleaning will be needed than stated here. Nets are normally re-impregnated once or twice a year after cleaning. Several Norwegian

Fig 49. Preparing to change a fouled net. (*Photograph: Arne Kittelsen*).

companies manufacture special anti-fouling compounds, the exact recipes of which are trade secrets but the bases of which are copper. The preparations can be used alone, but one major supplier claims better results by mixing 25% white spirit and 20% carbolinium with the fluid. Nets are soaked for about half an hour, then drained and hung up to dry.

Most of the marine fouling forms close to the surface, in the top two metres of net. Some farmers extend the interval between net changes by periodically pulling this part of the net out of the water. With eight-sided nets of about 5 m depth, the top two metres on one side can be pulled up without reducing the volume of the cage very much. The farmer hooks one side up and leaves it for a few days in the air, after which the fouling organisms have died and can be shaken off. That side is then lowered and the next side pulled up, and so on until the whole net has been worked round.

MOORING

Floating net cages must obviously be anchored to prevent them drifting away or being washed up onto the shore. Development of cage design in Norway has been by trial-and-error, and the same applies to mooring arrangements. There are, therefore, few hard-and-fast rules which can be laid down. Nevertheless, it is generally accepted that each six or eight-sided cage should be moored by at least three of its corners to prevent it blowing over in strong winds, while four-sided cages are often only attached by two of their (diagonally opposite) corners.

The method of anchoring depends on the way the cages are to be worked in the particular fish farm. Basically, cages can be arranged in three possible ways: (a) moored singly, as is the case in the majority of Norwegian fish farms (*Fig* 50), (b) several cages grouped together to form a raft, sometimes around a working platform, or (c) moored to either side of a floating walkway extending out from the shore (*Fig* 51).

Cages independent of the shore. Where cages are moored singly, or in groups without a working platform, it is highly desirable to have a quay to which the nets can be towed for maintenance work and fish harvesting. If young fish are brought to the farm by road such a quay is essential, as the tank-truck must be able to get near enough to each cage to pour fish straight in without intermediate handling. If young fish are delivered by boat a quay is still very useful, but a stable working platform which provides a secure working surface is an alternative. However, some farms have neither a quay nor a working platform, and in these all maintenance and harvesting work must be done from a boat. In farms with singly-

Fig 50. Floating net cages moored singly.

Fig 51. Net cages moored to a floating walkway. (*Photograph: Arne Kittelsen*).

95

moored or grouped nets all feeding must be done either by boat or by independent automatic feeders (see Chapter 8).

Usually, a number of cages share anchoring lines. To avoid imposing excessive strains, the principle is not to attach the anchoring line direct to the cage frame itself, but rather to have independent well-anchored lines (preferably two at right angles) to buoys in which each cage is fixed. The anchored lines frequently terminate either in ship's anchors or concrete blocks on the sea bed. However, where possible they are fixed to secure moorings on the shore via chains running on the bottom of the sea or suspended in mid-water underneath buoys.

The quantity of anchoring needed obviously depends on local conditions of tide and current flow. Some units move their surface position by more than 50 m as the direction of tidal flow changes and the slack in the mooring lines is taken up. Provided there is no obstruction to shipping this movement can be a good thing, as it spreads the waste from the cages over a wider area and thereby lessens the chance of oxygen depletion developing.

Floating walkways. By far the most convenient arrangement to work is that of nets moored to a floating walkway. Here access on foot is easy at any time, more frequent hand-feeding is possible, and no boat is required for day-to-day work. However, such a long floating structure offers a lot of surface area for wind and waves to operate on, and it must be strongly made and well anchored if it is not to prove a danger both to the cages it services and the men who work on it. Consequently floating walkways are expensive to install, and are at present used only in a minority of farms.

The Fish Breeding Experimental Station at Averøy near Kristiansund, which annually produces about 40 tonnes of fish for sale to the market as well as carrying out research, has its cages moored to two floating walkways (*Fig* 51). Each is about 90 m long, and the two join near the shore, to which they share a common access ramp. Each walkway is made up of sections, hinged together end to end by galvanized shackles. In addition a safety chain runs along the whole length of each walkway. Each section is constructed of a timber platform surmounting the flotation units, which are expanded polystyrene-filled fibreglass tanks. The sections of one of the walkways are 2×4 m, with a nett buoyancy of $125 \, \text{kg/m}^2$, and those of the other are 1.5×4 m and of $100 \, \text{kg/m}^2$ buoyancy. The buoyancy is sufficient to safely support the weight of two men plus a loaded food trolley.

The walkway sections are moored and stabilized by a system of chains and weights underneath (*Fig* 52). Under each section two static concrete weights lie on the sea bed. From each weight galvanized chains extend up to pulley wheels, one fixed on each side underneath the floating section.

96

The chain from each anchor weight passes through the pulley on either side, and the two chains meet and join at a counterweight suspended in mid-water underneath the walkway. As the walkway rises and falls with the tide, and with load in use, the counterweight moves up and down in the water, always maintaining tight chains between the anchor blocks and the pulleys.

To resist lateral forces of wind and currents, a heavy galvanized chain is attached to each walkway near its end. The chain runs out sideways on the sea bed to the shore at either side, where it is firmly attached in concrete. Two other chains link the walkways to the shore at intervals along the floating structures.

A total of 26 floating net cages, of various types and sizes between 200 and 500 m³, are normally moored to the walkways. In addition there are 24 small (3m × 3m × 3m) rectangular cages for special experimental purposes and for holding brood fish during stripping. The framework of each floating cage is secured to the walkway at two points with nylon rope or galvanized chain and, in the case of Grøntvedt-type cages, the frames are fended off with old vehicle tyres. The outer side of each cage, *ie* the side away from the walkway, is anchored to a concrete block on the sea bed. A buoy is inserted in the anchor line (*Fig* 52) to allow for tidal rise and fall without putting a direct strain on the cage frame itself. The outer anchors of the cages also serve to further anchor the walkway itself against lateral forces.

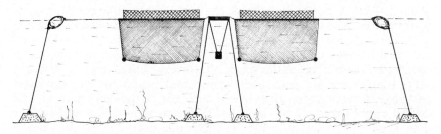

Fig 52. Mooring arrangement for the floating walkway and net cages at the Fish Breeding Experimental Station, Averøy. (*From Gjedrem, 1974*).

SITE SELECTION

Most sea water salmonid farms using floating net cages around the Norwegian coast are small, or at least had small beginnings. Most were started by fishermen or land farmers, initially on a part-time basis. As a result, few farms occupy the sites they do because the conditions there are especially favourable, but rather because the stretch of water happened to be near land belonging to a man who became interested in fish farming. The choice of site for most of these men was limited to the water in their own locality. Little formal survey work was normally done before the farm was established, the farmer merely installed a few floating nets and tried his site out. Some people may consider this a recipe for financial disaster, and of course some sites have proved unsuitable and the operation has ceased. However, the costs of trying a site out on a small scale, even if all the stock is lost, are probably no more than those of a full professional survey. Furthermore, if the site proves suitable, the trial-and-error approach has produced both a crop of fish and valuable experience for the novice farmer, whereas the survey has produced no financial gain, at least not to the farmer.

Of course, to say that no formal survey was done for most farm sites does not mean that no site selection was done at all. No farmer would place his floating cages in a completely exposed position, in a place which freezes over each winter, or where there is no current or tidal flow to effect water exchange. These and other qualitative site requirements were discussed in Chapter 5. However, it is extremely difficult to lay down hard-and-fast quantitative rules about what disqualifies a potential site from consideration, since farms sited apparently in contravention of the rules but nevertheless operating at a good profit can always be found. For example, it is a good general rule that an area of open water of more than about 2–3 km on the windward side of a unit permits sufficient build-up of waves to make the site unsuitable for floating cages (eg Braaten and Sætre, 1973). But the author has visited successful units on days when the wind has been howling down on flotillas of cages across many kilometres of open water. Similarly, in the south of Norway, where tidal currents are very weak, there are successful farms sited inside bays where water exchange is much poorer than would normally be thought necessary. Of course, cage culture is a new industry, and none of the farms cited is older than about 10 years. It could be that once every 20 or 30 years a sufficiently strong wind will arise to break up the cages in the first example. Similarly, over many years build-up of waste material around the cages may reach such a point that de-oxygenation will kill all fish in the farms in the second example. On the other hand our understanding of exactly what constitutes a suitable site is also imperfect, and local variations in conditions are very important. In some cases it would take many years of expensive measurement to decide, with a scientific 95% probability of being right, whether or not a particular local site is suitable for the long-term operation of a fish farm. Meanwhile most of the men who took a little greater chance of failure, and started in business based on their own local knowledge, are making profits.

OPERATION OF FLOATING CAGE UNITS

The sequence of production of both salmon and rainbow trout in sea cages was outlined in Chapter 2. Briefly, rainbow trout are stocked out either in spring, in which case they are harvested in autumn $1\frac{1}{2}$ years later, or in autumn, for harvest one year later. Salmon are stocked out in spring and harvested two years later.

Stocking density

Most salmon smolts, and many rainbow trout fingerlings, arrive at the fish farms by boat (Chapter 4). The boat steams right up to the nets, the hold valves are closed, and water is pumped out from the hold until the fish are confined in a relatively small space. The fish are then transferred from the hold to the cages with dip nets. Nets are composed of fine, smooth-meshed netting which is gentle to the delicate small fish. Sometimes the bottom of the dip net is lined with polythene sheeting so that fish are transferred in water as an extra precaution against damage. Fish are either counted by eye as they are poured from the net into a cage, or pass down a sloping counting board (*Fig* 53). Counting boards are covered with polythene sheeting to avoid abrasion to fish, and a small water jet from a hose at the top of the board keeps the fish wet.

When fish arrive by road each cage must be towed in to a quay onto which the truck can reverse. The outflow valve of the fish tank is simply opened and the fish and water it contains flow into the cage.

Stocking density of fish used in each cage is frequently 10–15 kg of fish/m^3 of cage at harvest, but up to 20 kg/m^3 or even more can safely be used if water circulation is good and nets are kept clean. Occasionally the farmer calculates right at the start how many fish he must stock in a cage to give this final crop at harvest, working from his experience of the average size each fish is likely to reach and the percentage expected to die between stocking and harvest. More usually, he initially stocks higher numbers of young fish than this in each cage and then grades the fish out into other cages later, after they have grown a little. In either case, most farmers like to remove samples of fish from their cages at intervals and weigh them to keep a check on the rate of growth. When fish are handled scales are inevitably knocked off and small wounds result through which disease organisms can gain entry to the fish. Therefore unnecessary

Fig 53. Smolts are counted from a live-hauling boat into a net cage using a polythene-covered board. One man represents the buyer and the other the seller.

handling is avoided and it is unusual to grade fish more than twice between stocking and harvest.

Routine work

The most arduous routine work is feeding, and this is discussed separately in Chapter 8.

Dead fish. Any dead fish should be removed from the cages at least once a week. Sometimes dead fish float. Even when they sink to the bottom of the net their silver sides make them easily visible, whereas the live fish in the net with their dark backs uppermost are frequently invisible. A long-handled dip net is useful for removing dead fish.

There are always some deaths from unexplained causes but if many fish die, or if their feeding or other behaviour changes for no apparent reason, a qualified fish pathologist should be consulted. Disease apart, mortality rate of fish between stocking and harvest varies with the husbandry skill of the farmer, but losses of up to one third are common.

Oxygen. It is advisable for farmers to check the level of dissolved oxygen in their cages at intervals, though few yet do this on any regular basis. Especially in units which use wet food, many wild fish of various species are attracted to the nets and can easily be seen by the farmer. While these are around he can be fairly sure that there is no shortage of oxygen in the water. If they suddenly disappear, however, the dissolved oxygen concentration should quickly be checked. Incidentally these wild fish include valuable flatfish and even wild salmon, and can provide a useful extra source of income for small farmers who catch them with hooks or nets.

Many farms using floating cages are experiencing a build-up of mud underneath the cages. This represents an accumulation of waste food and fish faeces and is rich in organic matter which uses oxygen as it decays. The possibility has been mentioned above that the oxygen demand of the mud could reach a high enough level for the water near the cages to become de-oxygenated and the fish stock to be killed. This has rarely happened so far, but it is a possibility that every farmer should bear in mind and make contingency plans for, so that he can act quickly to save his stock in the event of an emergency. In the short term most farms, which are small, could temporarily alleviate a crisis by towing cages away to a new site, or by circulating clean water around the cages using the propeller of a boat. However, in the long term it may be necessary in some cases to install sludge pumps, which can suck up the mud and water from under the cages and discharge it at a safe distance from the unit.

Maintenance. Cage mooring ropes, buoys and anchors must be checked at intervals for wear and replaced if necessary. Fouled nets must be changed, cleaned and re-impregnated.

Harvest

Farmers who grow salmon from smolt to harvest work on a two-year production cycle, and those producing rainbow trout in the conventional way use a $1\frac{1}{2}$ year cycle with some empty cages for a further half year. To obtain annual production and income such farmers will normally harvest from around 50–75% of their cages each year, the other 25–50% holding younger fish. After harvest these young fish are graded out into the 50–75% cages to be grown for slaughter the following year, and the 25–50% are re-stocked with new smolts or fingerlings. On the other hand a farmer using the one-year cycle of production for rainbow trout harvests from and re-stocks all his cages each autumn.

Harvesting fish from a floating cage is simple. The net is pulled up until the fish are confined in a small volume of water, from which they are removed by dip nets. In units with walkways, or where cages can be towed to a quay for harvest, shore-based power-driven hoists are often used to

H

operate large dip nets (*Fig* 54). These can also be used where cages are serviced by a large boat. However, in many units harvesting must be done from a small boat, and then a hand dip net is used and harvesting is much slower and more laborious (*Figs* 55 and 56).

EVALUATION OF CAGE CULTURE

In 1976, out of a total of around 200 significant sea water fish farms in Norway over 90% were floating cage units. In operation, the use of floating cages gives the farmer good control over his stock. Fish can easily be removed from cages at harvest, for pathological examination or weight sampling. Water exchange for floating cages is by natural water currents. They do not require the expensive pumping equipment and power necessary for most fixed units.

The biggest disadvantages of cages are their shorter working life and greater susceptibility to storm damage than most fixed, concrete units.

The main reason for the overwhelming popularity of cage culture, however, is the low cost of the basic equipment. A standard commercially-made floating cage, complete with net bag, can be bought for about

Fig 54. Harvesting fish from a net cage at a quay using a power hoist.

102

Fig 55. Harvesting fish from a net cage by hand from a small boat. (*Photograph: T Skretting A/S*).

NKr 8,000 (January 1977). An aspiring farmer prepared to make his own framework can buy a net bag only for around NKr 2,000. The floating cage method of production is an extremely flexible system, in the sense that successful farms can be established to produce any amount of fish required; the lower limit is one cage, and there is virtually no upper limit. In Norway, unit size varies from one-man part-time operations with only two or three nets up to fairly large-scale production in 60 or more nets, but there are no 'giants'. Furthermore, cage culture is a business in which an enterprising man can start small with little capital and expand gradually by adding more cages as his success grows. By comparison, all fixed units for producing salmonids in sea water (Chapter 6) require large amounts of capital for construction work, up to many millions of kroner for Mowi-type units, before any production can start. This is not to say that fixed units are not excellent systems once in operation, but it does mean that only large companies can afford the initial investment needed. In view of the recent government limit of 8,000 m³ imposed on the size of new fish farms (Chapter 1), all new units for the culture of salmonids in sea water are likely to be of the floating cage type for the foreseeable future.

Fig 56. Landing rainbow trout harvested in a small boat.
(*Photograph: T Skretting A/S*).

8 Food and Feeding

This chapter concentrates on practical diets and the methods by which they are delivered to the fish in Norwegian salmon and rainbow trout farms. Many of the diets used have been developed largely by trial and error. Scientific knowledge of the precise dietary requirements of salmonids is incomplete, and almost all experimentation has been done with small fish; research results from large fish as grown in Norway are very sparse. Therefore only a brief theoretical discussion is included here. (For further information on the known nutritional requirements of fish the reader should consult a standard text-book on the subject, *eg* Halver, 1972).

THEORY

Energy is required at all stages in the life cycle of all animals, including fish. It is used in movement, growth, reproduction, and for 'maintenance' *ie* all the chemical processes in the body required to keep the animal 'ticking over' even when it is at rest. Energy is often measured in calories, but these are small units and for animal food studies the term kcal (1,000 calories) is usually used, though it is now, strictly speaking, more correct to use joules instead of calories (1 joule = 0.239 cal). 1 kcal is the amount of heat required to increase the temperature of 1 kg of water by one degree celsius (°C). A fish must obtain all the energy it needs from its food, so the energy content is used as a basic measure of the value of particular foodstuffs.

Foods are composed basically of three types of chemical constituent; protein, fat and carbohydrate. When any of these compounds is broken down into simpler substances energy is released. Protein gives an average of 5.65 kcal/g, fat 9.45 kcal/g, and carbohydrate 4.0 kcal/g. However, these are total (or gross) calories, and are not all available to fish. The amount a fish can use depends on its ability to digest the constituents of the food, the energy in food which is not digested being lost with the faeces. In studies on salmonid fishes, the figures derived by Phillips and Brockway (1959) for estimating calorific value of dietary constituents for brook trout are often used. From previous studies they knew that protein was 90% digested (Tunison *et al.*, 1942), fat 85% digested (McCay and Tunison, 1935), and carbohydrate (starch) 40% digested (Phillips *et al.*, 1948). From this they calculated that protein in food provided 3.9 kcal of available energy per gram, fat 8.0 kcal/g, and carbohydrate (starch) 1.6 kcal/g. These are average figures and, for example, if more easily digestible sugars such as glucose or sucrose were present in the diet as well as starch, the available energy from carbohydrate would be much greater than stated here. These figures are the ones used by fish food manufacturers to calculate the 'available' or 'metabolizable' energy quoted in the advertising literature for their foods.

Basically, what the fish farmer wants is for his fish to grow as fast as possible on as little expense for food as possible. Next to water, the biggest constituent of fish flesh is protein. Some fat is also present, and indeed a high fat content is considered desirable for salmon and trout on the Norwegian market especially if the fish are to be smoked, but little carbohydrate is present. Also, generally speaking, fats and carbohydrates suitable for inclusion in salmonid diets are cheaper than protein per calorie of available energy they provide. The aim of the fish farmer or fish food producer, therefore, is to allow the fish to convert as high a percentage as possible of the protein in the food into fish flesh. Calories obtained by the fish by breaking down protein are expensive, and the objective is to give the fish calories sufficient to satisfy as high a percentage of its energy requirements as possible from fat and carbohydrate.

However, the digestive systems of salmonids are naturally equipped to handle foods consisting largely of protein, and their ability to utilize fat and carbohydrate is limited. A diet containing more of these substances than the fish can burn up to provide energy can cause mortality, frequently by damaging the liver. Opinions differ as to how much fat and carbohydrate salmon or trout can efficiently utilize. In commercially produced diets recent trends have been towards higher fat content, and up to 20% (of dry weight) is now used. Traditionally, very little carbohydrate is fed to salmonids, but again the recent trend has been to use more, and anything up to about 26% is now included in pelleted foods. Protein content in commercially produced diets is usually 40–50%.

Certain of the amino acids, of which proteins are composed, cannot be synthesized by salmonids and must be present in sufficient quantity in the diet. Proteins from animal and vegetable sources do not contain all the same amino acids, and the natural diet of salmonids contains mostly animal protein. In artificial diets a proportion of the animal protein can be replaced by cheaper vegetable ones, but it cannot all be replaced due to the fishes' requirement for essential amino acids only present in proteins of animal origin. Similarly, essential fatty acids, of which fats are composed, must be present in the diet, as must a number of vitamins and minerals.

PRACTICAL DIETS

The diets used in Norwegian salmon and trout farms are of two types:

(1) *Wet diets*, which are prepared at the fish farm by the farmer himself. These are basically minced wet fish, with added vitamins, minerals and binder.

(2) *Dry diets*. These are commercially manufactured complete foods, produced in factories and sold to the fish farmer in a ready-to-use, dry pelleted form.

The 'moist pellets' sometimes used in the USA, intermediate between wet and dry diets, are not employed in Norway.

WET DIETS

Wet diets are now used only for growing-on fish in sea water up to harvest size and for brood stock in either fresh or sea water.

Composition of wet foods

Fish. The basic constituent of wet diets is either whole industrial fish, or waste from the fish processing industry *ie* the heads, bones, viscera, skin *etc* left after the fish have been filleted. Fish species used as salmon and trout food can be divided into two groups: oily fish and 'white' (or non-oily) fish.

Oily fish have a high fat content in their muscles. Care must be taken in storing these species, since fat deteriorates quickly and rancid fat may make the fish unacceptable or even harmful to salmonids. Nevertheless, a few of the oily fishes are now the most used species as wet food for salmon or trout. By far the most common is the capelin (*Mallotus villosus*). These are small fish landed in very large quantity by the Norwegian fleet, being taken especially when they approach the coast of Finnmark in the north of Norway to spawn. Capelin are little used for human consumption, but much of the catch is converted to fish meal and oil for animal feeds. Other species of oily fish commonly used are sprats (*Clupea sprattus*), and sand-eels (*Ammodytes lancea* and *A. tobianus*). Other species are used in smaller quantities when the preferred ones are not available.

Almost any species of white fish can be used as salmonid food, but the most common are cod (*Gadus morhua*), coalfish (*Pollachius virens*), and other fishes of the cod family. As these fish are used for human consumption only the waste after filleting is available for use as salmonid food.

The protein content of whole fish is frequently around 17–18% of wet weight. Fat content in oily species varies widely according to species and season between about 4 and 20%. Capelin, for example, frequently contain 13–14% fat just before spawning in January–February, falling to 4–6% after spawning, the annual mean being around 10%. For non-oily species a fat content of 1–2% is usual.

When white fish is used as the basis of wet diets the prepared food frequently has a very low fat (around 5% on a dry weight basis) and high protein (over 80% of dry weight) content. Though growing satisfactorily on it, fish fed such a diet will have to break down much of the protein to satisfy their energy requirements. It is often economic, therefore, to add extra fat to the mixture to reduce the protein/fat ratio. The fat can be used by the salmon or trout to fill part of their energy requirement, leaving most of the protein free to be used for growth. Capelin oil is the most frequently used fat source for this purpose, and can be added at the rate of 2–6% of the wet food. Wet food mixtures based on oily fish normally already contain a high enough proportion of fat.

Where possible, the salmon farmer likes to feed his fish on the same industrial species all the time. This is because salmon are rather fussy about the taste of their food. If they are accustomed to eating, for example, capelin, and shortage of supply of this species suddenly necessitates changing over to coalfish, salmon will frequently refuse the new food and starve themselves for weeks. Rainbow trout are less fussy, but neverthe-less some temporary reduction in food consumption can still be expected if the diet is abruptly changed. Where a farmer knows that supply of any one species may be erratic he will try to feed a mixture of species all the time, so that the omission of one of them will not change the taste of the food completely.

Fish for use as salmonid food arrives at the farms in frozen blocks either by boat or truck (*Fig* 57). Some farms have deep-freeze storage facilities where they can keep supplies to last several weeks, but this is expensive both in capital outlay and power. Most farms instead rely on getting regular deliveries of industrial fish every few days. A/S Mowi of Bergen, for example, requires about 15 tonnes of industrial fish daily to feed the salmon in its two sea enclosures. This company has a contract for a special ship to deliver 25 tonnes four times a week.

Additives. Good results have been obtained in fish farms by feeding only whole capelin, and salmon are said to prefer the taste of this species. However, it is usual to complete wet diets by the addition of shrimp waste to give pink colour to the salmon or trout flesh (discussed below), a binder

Fig 57. Frozen blocks of industrial fish for use as salmon food. (*Photograph: A/S Mowi*).

to improve the consistency of the diet and stop it breaking up into small pieces, and vitamin and mineral additives to ensure that the diet is not deficient in any essential trace element. There is no difference between wet diets for rainbow trout and those for salmon.

Binding meals are commercially produced in a variety of different formulations. Some only serve the basic function of holding the food together better to reduce wastage. These are frequently added to the food at a rate of about 1%. Others contain all the vitamins and minerals necessary for the fish, so that these need not be added separately, and about 5–10% of this meal is added to the food. Meals with flesh-colouring pigments are also available. All binding meals are largely composed of carbohydrate, containing 10% or less protein and about 3% fat.

Feeding with wet food

On the majority of fish farms wet food is delivered to the salmon or trout by hand. However, in a few farms semi-mechanized methods are used. Different consistencies of food are required for machine and hand feeding. For hand feeding the food must be in discrete pieces of about the right size for the fish to take in one bite. For use in machines food requires a much smoother, stickier consistency suitable for extrusion through an aperture which automatically determines the size of particle produced.

Hand feeding. Hand feeding is employed in almost all floating cage units which use wet food. The industrial fish, shrimp shells, binding powder and vitamin mix (powder or liquid), are simply put together in the hopper of an electrically driven mincing machine and coarsely minced. Before they go into the mincer the frozen blocks of fish are either thawed sufficiently to separate individual fish, or are chopped up with an axe. The food is usually allowed to fall from the nozzle of the mincer into plastic containers (*Fig* 58). These are loaded onto a boat in the case of units using individually moored cages, or onto a trolley where cages are moored to a floating walkway, for transport to the cages. The food is manually thrown into the cages using a shovel or hand scoop (*Fig* 59).

It is possible to calculate approximately how much food a given weight of fish 'should' eat per day. But as this varies so much according to mean size of fish, water temperature and weather conditions, and a farmer rarely knows precisely what weight of fish he has in a cage anyway, most people prefer to feed according to appetite, *ie* as long as the fish eagerly accept food the farmer will try to supply it. Wet food tends to float or sink only slowly, so it is easy to observe whether fish are eating it.

Most farmers feed their fish as often as possible, since it is believed that frequent feeding with small meals gives better growth than occasional

110

Fig 58. Preparing wet food with a mincer.

feeding with large meals. It certainly seems likely that food will have less time to drift out of the cage and be wasted if small meals are given. It is usual to give food only during daylight hours. For farms in the north of Norway, though, this means virtually 24 hours a day in summer. For example, at the farm of Mr Torrissen near Bodø, one of the largest salmon units in the country, the cages are moored in parallel rows and, in summer, a boat works continuously up and down between the rows feeding fish. On small farms, many of which are run by one man, feeding is less frequent. When the unit is run as a part-time business only, fish feeding of course has to be fitted in around the owner's other job. Satisfactory growth rates

111

Fig 59. Feeding salmon with wet food by hand. (*Photograph: Arne Kittelsen*).

can, however, be obtained by feeding only once or twice a day.

Feeding by machine. The preparation of wet food to be fed out automatically is best illustrated by the example of A/S Mowi, by far the most important company using this system. Mowi's two sea enclosures were described in Chapter 6. All food is prepared at the larger unit at Veløykjølpo. There, the frozen blocks of industrial fish are thawed in special outdoor tanks (*Fig* 60). The water pumped into these tanks has a temperature over 6° C even in winter because it is drawn from deep in the sea. The thawed fish is transported on a conveyor belt into a food preparation building, where it falls into a large mincing machine. Shrimp waste is added via another conveyor belt. The minced food then passes into a blending machine, where fish meal powder, binder and a vitamin and mineral mixture of Mowi's own recipe are added. This machine turns the food into a thick, sticky paste, which falls into polythene transport containers. The containers are moved by fork-lift truck either direct to the feeders at Veløykjølpo, or onto boats (*Fig* 61) for transport to the company's other sea enclosure at Flogøykjølpo.

The feeding system used at both units is the same, and was specially designed by the company. Prepared food is put into a stainless steel hopper, and an electrically driven screw at the bottom expels food through a nozzle in a continuous 'worm'. Spokes projecting from the rim of a revolving wheel cut the worm into wet pellets as it emerges from the nozzle, and the size of pellet can be varied by changing the speed of revolution of the cutting wheel. The pellets drop into a long plastic drain pipe which extends on floats out into the sea enclosure. A small electric pump discharges water into the top of the pipe so that the pellets are washed along and out onto the water surface in the enclosure. Water current from an electrically driven propeller mounted on a float nearby

Fig 60. Frozen blocks of industrial fish are thawed in tanks of sea water before being minced for feeding to salmon. (*Photograph: A/S Mowi*).

113

Fig 61. Prepared wet food is transported to A/S Mowi's sea enclosure at Flogøykjølpo by boat in fibreglass tanks. The same type of tank is used to transport slaughtered fish.

distributes the food in a stream down the enclosure. Food is given continuously in daylight hours.

Wet food dispensers are in use at a few floating cage units, but are not common. One such feeding machine, driven by a power supply from the shore, is shown in *Fig* 62. Wet food, prepared with a blender, is put into the hopper, and a rotating arm at the bottom expresses the food through a slit.

DRY DIETS

Complete, dry diets are now used in all fresh water fish farms for growing young salmon up to the smolt stage of development, and rainbow trout up to 50–150 g, ready for stocking out into the sea. Dry food is also increasingly being used for growing-on fish in sea units right up to harvest, and in 1978 the tonnages of fish produced on wet and dry foods are expected to be about the same.

114

Two companies, T Skretting A/S of Stavanger, Norway, and Astra-Ewos A/B of Sweden, supply most of the dry food used in this country. Both companies manufacture 'salmon' and 'trout' foods, though in fact either can be used for both salmon and trout with satisfactory results. The crude chemical compositions of salmon and trout diets produced by the Norwegian manufacturer are shown in *Tables* 2 and 3. The main differences are higher proportions of protein and fat, and a higher calorie content, in the salmon food. Also, a higher proportion of the protein and fat is from marine animal sources. Salmon food contains more vitamins than trout food. Salmon foods cost about 10% more per calorie than trout foods, but it does seem that fish of both species grow faster on the more expensive food.

The composition of diets also varies according to the size of fish to be fed. Little fish are given a diet higher in both protein and energy content than that given to larger fish (*Tables 2 and 3*).

Food pellets (*Fig* 63) are made up in a range of sizes from finely ground powder for first feeding, through intermediate crumbles and small pellets, up to large pellets of about 1 cm diameter and $1\frac{1}{2}$ cm length. The manufacturers recommend which size of pellet should be given to which size of fish, and also produce feeding tables (*Table* 4) which advise approxi-

Fig 62. A wet food dispenser for use with a floating net cage.

115

mately how much food to give per unit number of fish of a given size at a given water temperature.

In the larger pellet sizes manufacturers provide a choice of foods for use in fresh or sea water, the latter containing less minerals. They also produce pigmented foods (see below) and medicated foods (Chapter 9).

Dry diets are not completely dry, and contain between 8 and 11% water. Only sinking pellets are used in Norway, the floating type popular in the USA is not used.

Constituents of dry foods

Exact recipes of commercially produced diets, and their vitamin additives, are trade secrets. However, an example of a dry food formulation which has proved experimentally to produce growth of young salmon as good as the major commercially produced foods used in Norway is shown in *Tables* 5 and 6.

The largest constituent of all Norwegian dry foods is 'herring' meal. In Norway this all comes through the Norwegian herring oil and herring

Fig 63. Dry, pelleted food for salmonids. (*Photograph: T Skretting A/S*).

116

Table 2. Crude chemical composition of pelleted rainbow trout feed. (By courtesy of T Skretting A/S)

	% protein min.	% fat min.	% nitrogen free components	Metabolizable energy kcal/kg min.	% protein animal/ vegetable	% fat marine/ vegetable
Starter feed size nos. 0, 1, 2	48	20	14	3700	86/14	88/12
Growth feed size nos. 3, 4	41	20	22	3550	83/17	85/15
Slaughter feed size nos. 4A, 5, 6, 7, 8	40	15	26	3200	66/34	80/20

Table 3. Crude chemical composition of pelleted salmon feed. (By courtesy of T Skretting A/S).

	% protein min.	% fat min.	% nitrogen free components	Metabolizable energy kcal/kg min.	% protein animal/ vegetable	% fat marine/ vegetable
Starter feed size nos. 0, 1, 2	51	20	10	3850	93/7	88/12
Growth feed size nos. 3, 4	48	20	14	3700	86/14	88/12
Slaughter feed size nos. 4A, 5, 6, 7, 8	41	20	22	3550	83/17	85/15

117

I

Table 4. Rainbow trout feeding table. (By courtesy of T Skretting A/S)

Feed type	Starter feed			Growth feed				Slaughter feed			
Feed size no.	0	1–2	2	3	3–4	4	4A	5	5–6	6	7–8
No. fish/kg	5000	5000–650	650–250	250–100	100–50	50–25	25–15	15–10	10–7	7–5	5–
Mean fish size (cm)	2.5	2–5.5	5–7.5	7.5–10	10–12.5	12.5–15	15–17.5	17.5–20	20–22.5	22.5–25	25–
Water temperature °C	*Daily feed quantity (kg/100 kg fish)*										
4	3.8	3.0	2.5	1.9	1.5	1.3	1.1	0.9	0.8	0.7	0.6
6	4.0	3.2	2.6	2.0	1.7	1.5	1.3	1.1	1.0	0.9	0.8
8	4.8	3.8	3.0	2.4	1.9	1.7	1.5	1.3	1.2	1.1	1.0
10	5.5	4.5	3.6	2.8	2.2	2.0	1.7	1.5	1.4	1.3	1.2
12	6.5	5.2	4.2	3.2	2.5	2.3	2.0	1.7	1.6	1.5	1.4
14	7.5	6.0	5.0	3.7	2.9	2.6	2.3	2.0	1.8	1.7	1.6
16	8.5	7.0	5.8	4.3	3.5	3.0	2.6	2.3	2.1	2.0	1.9
18	5.0	4.5	3.7	3.0	2.4	2.2	1.9	1.6	1.5	1.3	1.3
20	3.0	2.6	2.3	2.0	1.6	1.4	1.2	1.0	0.9	0.8	0.7
Min. no. of daily feedings	10	8	6			4			3	2	

118

meal sales organization 'Norsildmel', a state monopoly. Though called 'herring' meal, it is actually made mostly from capelin these days, but sprats, mackerel and herring are also used in smaller amounts. Herring meal contains over 70% protein and about 7% fat, and usually makes up between 30 and 50% of complete dry diets.

Animal products including blood meal (around 85% protein and 0.5% fat) and skimmed milk powder (35% protein, 52% carbohydrate, 0.6% fat) are often used in small amounts in dry salmonid diets. Many slaughter-house wastes are good fish food components but are expensive and rarely available in large enough quantities to be extensively used. Food components of vegetable origin are traditionally less used in salmonid foods, but protein-rich soya bean meal now forms between 10 and 30% of commercial diets. When high levels of soya meal are used the amount of fish meal in the food can be reduced, but never below 20%. A wide variety of plant products can be used in small amounts to add vegetable protein as well as carbohydrate to the diet.

Fat is added to increase the energy content of dry foods. Fish oil (frequently capelin or cod) or soya oil is used for this. Experiments have shown that growth of both young salmon and rainbow trout is improved with increased dietary fat content up to 16%, the highest level tested (Austreng, 1976a, b, c).

Table 5. Ingredients and chemical composition of the salmon feed formulation 'NLH 8' (from Austreng, 1976).

Ingredients	%	Chemical composition	
Mackerel meal	46.1	Dry matter %	91·1
Soyabean meal	13.8	Crude protein %	45.8
Skimmed milk powder	4.6	HCl-ether extract (fat) %	16.0
Blood meal	1.8	Crude fibre %	2.4
Dried brewer's yeast	3.7	N-free extracts %	16.7
Precooked wheat	4.6	Ash %	9.1
Wheat bran	7.7	Calcium %	1.27
Grass meal	1.8	Phosphorus %	1.23
Seaweed meal	1.8	Gross energy kcal/kg	4860
Soya oil	7.0	Metabolizable energy, kcal/kg	3340
Cod liver oil	3.52	ME from protein %	53.6
Lecithin	0.92	ME from fat %	38.4
Vitamin mixture I	0.92	ME from carbohydrate %	8.0
Salt	0.46	Animal protein of total protein %	78.2
Chalk meal	0.92	Lysine %	3.63
Micromineral mixture *	0.046	Methionine + cystine %	1.91
Methionine	0.092	Arginine %	2.75

* 21.4 mg Fe, 28.6 mg Mn, 25.2 mg Zn, 7.2 mg Cu, 0.5 mg Co, 1.0 mg I.

119

Vitamin		Mixture I (for small fish)	Mixture II (for larger fish)
Vitamin A	IU/kg	750 000	350 000
Vitamin D₃	IU/kg	150 000	70 000
Vitamin K₃	mg/kg	1 000	1 000
Alpha-tocopherol	mg/kg	25 000	6 200
Thiamine	mg/kg	2 500	6 600
Riboflavin	mg/kg	15 000	15 000
Pyrodoxine	mg/kg	4 500	2 200
Ca-pantothenate	mg/kg	5 500	5 500
Niacin	mg/kg	55 000	55 000
Folic acid	mg/kg	1 000	1 000
Vitamin B₁₂	mg/kg	1	1
Biotin	mg/kg	45	45
Choline chloride	mg/kg	350 000	110 000
Inositol	mg/kg	55 000	—
Paraminobenzoic acid	mg/kg	2 500	—
Ascorbic acid	mg/kg	26 500	26 500

Delivery and storage of pelleted foods

Dry, pelleted foods are usually delivered to the fish farm by truck but sometimes by boat. Most commonly, the pellets are packed at the factory in multi-layered paper sacks with polythene linings, and sacks are delivered stacked on wooden pallets. Crumbles and small pellets often come in 25 kg sacks, larger pellets in 50 kg sacks. However, for large pellets bulk delivery is gaining popularity, the food being transferred from a road tanker into a tall storage hopper at the customer's farm (*Fig* 64). Bulk delivery is cheaper because it saves packing and handling expense at the factory, and can also save labour on the farm. Hoppers can be conveniently sited right at the water's edge so that their outlet chutes can be swung over the water to discharge pellets directly into a boat. There is a little more wastage of food by crushing to powder (or 'fines') in bulk handling, but a sieve screen can be fitted at the hopper outlet to remove and save powder. Sometimes the manufacturer will credit customers for the weight of powder returned; alternatively it can be used on the farm as an ingredient in wet foods.

Pelleted food in sacks should be stored in a cool, dry place raised off the ground on pallets (*Fig* 65). Properly stored, it will keep well for 3–4 months in summer or 6–7 months in winter. In cold storage it is good for up to 12 months. It is, however, recommended that dry foods should be bought in smaller amounts and used quickly rather than large amounts to be stored for a long time on the farm, as some deterioration inevitably occurs with time.

Feeding with dry food

Water temperature is the most important factor determining how much food fish will eat. Consumption increases with temperature within the range in which the fish are 'happy', but at high temperatures approaching

Fig 64. A hopper for bulk storage of dry food pellets.

121

Fig 65. Paper sacks of dry food are stored on wooden pallets.

the limits of tolerance food consumption declines. The feeding tables produced by the manufacturers of dry foods (*Table* 4) give a guide to the amount of food which young fish require. However, with fry it is usual to supply more food to the fish than they will eat. This is because the farmer wants his fish to grow as fast as possible, so that they are ready for transfer to the sea as early as possible. For very small fish the cost of the extra food given above what the fish eat is small compared with the costs of equipment, labour, and other overheads, and the price is worth paying to ensure that food is always available to the fish when they want it. For larger fish being grown-on either in fresh water, or more usually the sea, it is normal to feed according to appetite as with wet food.

All fresh water farms producing small fish in Norway are now equipped with automatic feeders. These were initially installed to save labour, but for fry it has now been demonstrated experimentally that, within limits, fish will grow more on a certain weight of food if it is given in many small meals rather than a few large ones. Automatic feeders are frequently set to deliver food about every 15 minutes during daylight hours. Where fish are kept indoors, artificial lighting is operated by a time switch. Lights are kept on for up to 24 hours each day, during which time the fish are fed. On the contrary, in most sea units which grow fish on to harvest, feeding is done by hand. Pellets are thrown to fish in the same way and with the same frequency as described above for wet food. However, automatic feeders for use with floating net cages are commercially available, and are successfully used in a number of units.

Wherever automatic feeders are used for fish bigger than fry, in fresh water or the sea, it is usual to set the machines to deliver approximately 75% of the daily ration. The other 25% is given by hand according to appetite. Hand feeding is important as it allows the culturist to observe the behaviour of his fish.

Some fish farms use both dry and wet foods. In this case wet food is given during working hours, when the labour is on hand to prepare it, and dry food for the rest of the day and during holidays using automatic feeders.

Automatic feeders

Demand feeders, *ie* automatic feeders from which food delivery is triggered by the fish themselves, are not popular in Norway, though a few are used in fresh water units growing rainbow trout in ponds. However, the vast majority of feeders used are of the timed type, from which food is delivered in amounts and at intervals pre-determined by the fish farmer.

All timed automatic feeders consist basically of a hopper, in which food pellets are put, surmounting a trigger device which releases or shoots out some of the pellets each time it fires. Several different types of triggering systems are commercially available, and they can conveniently be considered in groups according to the power source they use. These are:

(*1*) 12 or 24 volt units receiving their power by wires through a transformer from the mains electricity supply.

(*2*) Compressed air driven units, the compressed air being supplied by an electric or diesel-powered compressor.

(*3*) Units operated by individual re-chargeable dry batteries.

(*4*) A few fish farms have developed their own 'home-made' systems.

Electrically powered feeders. Automatic feeders working on low voltage electric power are the most popular for use indoors with fry tanks or raceways. The feeding control system has four parts:

(*a*) A time switch connected directly to an earthed mains socket (in Norway 220v, 50 Hz). This is used to switch the whole system off at night.

(*b*) A transformer, which reduces the voltage from 220 to 12, or more often 24, AC. This is much safer for use near water.

(c) A control unit, which can be adjusted to deliver electrical impulses at any desired interval and for the desired duration of time, ie pulse frequency and length. The feeders will release food each time the impulse is supplied and for as long as it is continued.

(d) Wire connections from the control unit to the feeders, and the feeders themselves.

Modern control units can be fitted with electronic eyes, which automatically switch the system on at dawn and off at dusk, or on and off as the artificial lights are used. However, it is still useful to have the time switch in the system to manually override this. Each fish tank has its own feeder, and large tanks frequently have more than one. Therefore, although one control unit will operate up to 20 feeders, quite a number of these units are needed for large smolt or fingerling barns (Fig 66).

Several different types of electrically driven feeders are sold in Norway, but only the two most widely used will be described here. For a number of years Astra-Ewos A/B has produced a popular feeder, the triggering device of which is an electric motor which turns a disc through a system of gears (Fig 67). Food in the hopper falls by gravity on to the top of the horizontal disc, and the amount which spills out onto the plate can be adjusted by changing the gap between the bottom edge of the cylindrical hopper and the disc. This gap is also increased to accommodate larger pellets. The electric motor is underneath the centre of the disc, and each time an impulse from the control unit is received the disc turns by a pre-set amount. An angled metal plate pushes food off the disc into the water below. Each time the disc turns, metal spokes inside the hopper cylinder near its bottom turn to prevent the food pellets sticking together and failing to run. These feeders are clamped to the sides of their fry tanks.

The second type of electrically driven fry feeder in common use in Norway is marketed by T Skretting A/S, and works on an entirely different principle from the Ewos unit. Electrical impulses are received by a vibrator situated just inside the opening at the bottom of the conical food hopper. Underneath the hopper is a small plastic disc, which is an integral part of the vibrator (Fig 68). Pellets fall by gravity onto the disc, which vibrates each time impulses are received from the control unit. Pellets are thrown off the disc into the water, and the vibrating action also ensures that pellets in the hopper are kept freely running. The feeder is adjusted for pellet size and amount of food delivered by turning a knob which makes the vibrator shake the disc more or less vigorously. These feeders are suspended by their electric cables above the water in the fish tanks.

Compressed air feeders. With large outdoor ponds and raceways, and sometimes with floating net cages, automatic feeders triggered by compressed air are often used. The most popular models used in Norway are

Fig 66. Electric control units for automatic fry-feeders.

Fig 67. An electrically driven fish feeder produced by Astra-Ewos A/B.

125

marketed by Astra-Ewos A/B. The components of a compressed air feeding system are:

(a) A compressor (*Fig* 69), the size of which depends on the number of feeders it is required to operate. For example, to run 20–25 feeders a compressor with a capacity of 200 litres of air per minute is required. Compressors are normally electrically powered, and require a high voltage (380v, 3-phase) supply. The compressor pressurizes an air chamber, the release of puffs of air from which drives the feeders.

(b) An electric control unit, which times and triggers the release of puffs of compressed air from the air chamber. The control unit runs on mains electricity, and can be set to fire the feeders at any frequency up to about four times per hour. The maximum rate of firing is dependent on the time taken by the compressor to build up sufficient pressure in the chamber. A time clock is also incorporated in the control unit so that the system can be shut down during the night. Both the compressor and control unit should be placed inside a building.

(c) High pressure air pipes running between the control unit and the individual feeders.

(d) The feeders themselves.

In the feeder units food pellets fall by gravity into a hole in the side of a

Fig 68. Vibrator-type feeders, sold by T Skretting A/S, hanging over fry tanks.

pipe, which is connected at one end to the compressed air line from the control unit. Its other end is open, and the pipe points out horizontally over the water like the barrel of a gun (*Fig* 70). When air is released by the control unit, the pellets in the pipe are blown out of the barrel and more fall in to take their place. Some feeders have a subsidiary air chamber on the feeder itself. The pellets are expelled from the barrel with some force, and can be shot several metres from the feeder. The number of pellets delivered each time the system fires can be adjusted by varying the gap through which they fall into the firing pipe, and this gap is also adjusted for pellet size. Compressed air feeders can be clamped to the sides of concrete ponds or raceways, or fixed to wooden catwalks over earth ponds or next to floating cages.

Independent battery driven feeders. Recently a new feeding system, designed by Sterner Aquaculture and sold in Norway by T Skretting A/S, appeared on the Norwegian market. The system is designed to be used with the Sterner floating cages described in Chapter 7, but it can be used with any type of cage or with ponds or tanks. The feeder is composed of two parts:

(*a*) The food hopper, into the bottom of which a vibrator and plastic disc similar to those described above for electrically driven feeders is

Fig 69. A central compressor used to drive 20 automatic feeders.

fixed. However, unlike those previously described, the vibrator runs on 12v DC.

(*b*) Electrical impulses are provided by a compact power source and control unit, all housed in a waterproof plastic casing the size of a flash-lamp. The complete unit weighs only half a kilo. The power source is a battery which requires re-charging every 1–3 months depending on usage. Besides control knobs by which pulse duration and frequency are easily adjusted, the control unit is equipped with an electric eye, so that operation automatically stops during the night. The control and battery unit is joined to the vibrator by a short length of waterproof cable, and fits neatly into a hole in the side of the food hopper. Therefore no wires are required to link the feeders to a central control unit; each operates entirely independently.

Hoppers are made of plastic and can be of any size required, a convenient one being the size of a dustbin. The whole unit is designed to hang from an aluminium tube across the middle of a floating cage (*Fig* 47).

'*Home-made' feeder systems.* These days there are plenty of excellent

Fig 70. A compressed air operated automatic feeder.

commercially made automatic feeders available, the ones most used in Norway being described above. However, in the early sixties when fish farming in Norway started this was not the case, and some farmers designed their own feeders. Only one example will be described here, that of A/S Mowi. At Mowi's biggest smolt unit, at Øyerhamn on the island of Varaldsøy in Hardangerfjord, there are 60 outdoor free-standing circular fibreglass tanks each of 3 m diameter. These are arranged in rows, and all the feeders to the tanks in each row are linked by a cable. At one end of the row the cable enters a small hut and is linked to a single electric control unit. When this fires it pulls the cable, which mechanically triggers the release of food from all the feeders. The cable is returned to its original position by a weight hanging on its free end.

A few units successfully operate water-powered automatic feeders, but low winter temperatures limit their use in Norway.

Comparison of different feeder types. The type of automatic feeder which is best depends, of course, on the location in which it must be used. For farms producing fry and fingerlings in small indoor tanks there is little doubt that centrally controlled electrically driven feeders deserve their premier position in the market. The disadvantage of this system for large ponds or raceways, however, is that the food is not spread over the water surface, but is all dropped in one place. This can be overcome by taking advantage of water currents. For example, Øksna Bruk A/S successfully uses electric feeders with earth ponds. The feeders are situated over the inlet channel to each pond, and the flow of incoming water serves to spread the pellets in a stream down the pond each time the feeder fires.

For outdoor use, however, many people prefer compressed air operated feeders. These spread the food over the water surface much better. One disadvantage of compressed air feeders is the noise, both of the compressor itself but more especially of released gas when the feeders fire. The latter can be quite alarming, especially when this type of feeder is used indoors. Freezing problems can also occur in the sub-zero air temperatures of a Norwegian winter. As air is compressed, together with its water vapour, it is heated greatly. When the control unit fires the air travels quickly down the pipes to the feeders, cooling rapidly as its pressure falls. Water sometimes condenses out of the air and freezes on feeder valves, thus stopping or reducing the efficiency of operation.

Despite the problems, it is possible to get some type of automatic feeder to work satisfactorily for all land-based fish farms whether they use tanks, ponds or raceways. In the sea, however, the problems are much greater. Most difficult of all is the necessity of having a link, either a cable or an air line, to a central control unit on shore. This is possible where floating net cages are moored to a floating walkway or very close to the shore, but in most Norwegian fish farms the cages are moored independently some distance from the shore. The recently introduced Sterner unit is currently the only independent automatic feeder system on the market, and the use of this unit or a development of it with floating net cages can be expected to increase in the future. Though this system can also be used with land based facilities, its cost would be high because a separate control unit is required for each feeder.

PIGMENTATION

At market, a red or pink-coloured flesh is considered essential in large salmon and rainbow trout. Colouring is caused by carotenoid pigments, and in nature the fish acquire these by eating crustacean animals containing the pigment astaxanthin. Some species of crustaceans are available to salmonids whether they live in fresh or sea water. In fresh water, for example, the well-known gammarus (*Gammarus lacustris* or *G. pulex*) is important, whilst in the sea a wide variety of shrimp-like organisms are present.

Under the artificial conditions in fish farms of the Norwegian type, however, almost all the food the fish get has to be supplied by the farmer, who must also supply the necessary pigments to colour the flesh. Salmon and rainbow trout cannot utilize vegetable pigments well, though these have been tried. One Norwegian fish farmer believed he had coloured the flesh of his fish to a nice pink by adding beetroot to their food. He was probably never fully convinced by the scientists' more likely explanation that the colour came from natural planktonic crustaceans which entered his floating cages from the surrounding sea. Unfortunately such natural pigment sources are not reliable.

Wet diets

It is usual to add shrimp waste, *ie* the heads, tails and shells of cooked shrimps or prawns, the bodies of which have been sold for human consumption, to wet diets. This is added at the rate of about 10% of the diet, which gives a concentration in the prepared food of about 5 or 6 ppm of astaxanthin.

Dry diets

In dry diets, the manufacturer offers a choice of pigmented or unpigmented food in the larger pellet sizes. Pigment is not added to fry foods.

Some crustacean waste may be added to pelleted diets, and the oil derived from capelin used in the manufacture of dry foods often contains some astaxanthin from the crustaceans in the stomachs of the small fish. However, most of the pigment added to dry foods is a related carotenoid called canthaxanthin. Though this pigment does occur naturally, that added to dry fish diets is artificially synthesized. Canthaxanthin is said to give a better, *ie* darker red, colour to the salmonid flesh, but is less stable than astaxanthin. Fish flesh coloured with canthaxanthin can become a little paler during processing, especially if the fish is boiled. Nevertheless canthaxanthin is a perfectly satisfactory and safe pigment, and fish coloured with this are not regarded as in any way inferior to those coloured with astaxanthin. In fact at market no-one could tell the difference. Around 40–60 ppm of canthaxanthin is added to pigmented dry foods.

Commercially produced binding meals containing canthaxanthin can be used as an alternative to shrimp waste in wet diets.

Feeding with pigmented food

It is not necessary to feed pigmented food, wet or dry, to salmonids for their whole lives, or even for the whole of their sea water lives. Some farmers do so, however, as a safety precaution. The farmer then knows that any fish requiring early slaughtering because of an emergency such as oxygen depletion will at least be saleable if their flesh is coloured. However, unless an emergency is considered likely, it seems extravagant to feed in this way. Pigments are expensive and add greatly to the cost of the foods which contain them.

Normally it is known approximately when fish will be harvested, and it is only necessary to give pigmented food for a few months immediately before slaughter. Canthaxanthin has to be given for a bit longer than astaxanthin to achieve the same degree of pigmentation. The time needed to develop the desired colour depends on water temperature, less time being needed at higher temperature. Generally, for rainbow trout harvested in autumn it is necessary to feed pigmented food for about three months, whilst for salmon harvested in spring up to six months is needed due to the lower water temperatures preceding harvest. Some companies do not harvest only at these 'conventional' times of year. For example A/S Mowi harvests some of its salmon all through their second year in the sea, partly to reduce stocking density in the sea enclosures and partly to take advantage of favourable market conditions (Chapter 6). In this and similar cases, therefore, it is necessary to feed pigmented food continuously after the fish have been in the sea for six months.

CONVERSION EFFICIENCY

Conversion efficiency obtained with the same food can vary enormously according to the method of feeding and the general skill of the fish farmer. For wet foods, containing about 12–1300 kcal of available energy/kg, conversions as low as 4 and as high as 16 to one have been reported, but the average is around 6 or 8:1. For dry foods, better (lower) conversions can be obtained with small fish up to about 50 g, and for these figures as low as 1:1 have been claimed with high energy foods (about 3670 kcal available energy/kg). For larger fish, conversions from $1\frac{1}{2}$ to 3:1 have been reported, but around 2:1 is normal both for salmon and rainbow trout.

COMPARISON OF WET AND DRY FOODS

Wet foods were traditionally used for growing-on salmonids in Norwegian sea water fish farms. They are still preferred by many fish farmers because they feel that they provide a more natural diet, and because experience over the years has proved that they produce satisfactory results. It has also been claimed that consumers preferred the taste of salmon fed on wet diets, but this was during the early days of the development of dry diets; modern dry foods probably produce fish with an equally good flavour as those fed on wet foods. Wet food may be more readily acceptable to the fish, and it is certainly easier to observe whether fish are feeding well or not on floating wet food than on sinking dry food. Though experiments conducted by the food manufacturers have shown that salmonids grow just as well on dry food the experience of many fish farmers, especially in the north of Norway, is that growth of salmon and trout is inferior on dry food at low temperatures (Chapter 12). If young salmonids are transferred directly from fresh to sea water there may be some temporary physiological advantage for them in receiving wet food with its higher water content.

Dry foods, on the other hand, have several advantages over wet. First, their composition and quality is much more reliable, and continual availability of the same food is guaranteed. Second, dry foods save a lot of labour. Even if feeding is not automated, pelleted diets eliminate the time consuming and messy job of food preparation required for wet food. Because of their lower water content, there is only about one third of the weight of food to carry out and deliver to the fish when dry diets are used. Delivery to the farm is also cheaper, since much less weight and bulk is involved. Thirdly, storage of dry food is much easier, and the farmer needs less frequent deliveries. He also has more peace of mind if bad weather hinders delivery, because enough dry food can always be kept on hand to tide him over. Fourthly, taking into account only the costs of wet and dry foods and the efficiency of their conversion into fish flesh, dry foods usually work out cheaper than wet per kilo of fish produced. When the saving in labour costs on the farm is also considered the differential in production cost between the two types of food is increased. However, locally some cost advantage may always remain in the use of wet foods by farmers in parts of northern Norway. There, most of the country's wet fish is landed, and prices are therefore lower than elsewhere. Pelleted food is currently produced only in southern Norway, and the delivery costs to the north can be high. In addition some farmers are currently able to obtain fish waste from processing plants for only the cost of transport.

On balance, dry foods often provide the most economical diets for farmed salmon and rainbow trout. If automated feeding systems for use with floating cages gain wide acceptance, and the problem of inferior fish growth at low temperature can be solved, the trend towards dry foods is likely to continue. In future the use of wet foods may become as unthinkable for sea water farms as it already is in fresh water fry and fingerling units.

K

9 Disease

Disease has not been a major limitation on the development of fish farming in Norway. Large numbers of parasite species are found occasionally on fish in farms, but few of these ever occur with sufficient incidence or intensity to be considered a problem. This chapter deals only with those pathogens which are sometimes a serious enough problem in Norwegian salmon and trout farms to require treatment. (For a fuller coverage of salmonid disease diagnosis the reader should consult a standard text-book, *eg* Roberts and Shepherd, 1974).

FRESH WATER

Husbandry conditions are of primary importance in determining whether or not diseases gain a hold on fish in a farm. Generally, conditions in Norwegian fresh water salmonid farms make them less prone to disease problems than their counterparts in most other countries. Earth ponds are relatively little used in Norway. Instead, most smolts or fingerlings are reared in plastic or concrete tanks, which are kept very clean and have rapid water turnover. These conditions eliminate the secondary hosts necessary for completion of the life cycles of many parasites, tend to flush away the infective stages of those pathogens which are present, and maintain a higher general water quality.

Disease organisms

Nevertheless disease organisms do sometimes occur, gaining entry to the farm in water supplies drawn from surface waterways containing wild fish. The most troublesome pathogens in Norway, in approximate order of importance, are:

Costia. This very small protozoan is found on the skin and gill surfaces of salmonids, especially fry. It occurs most commonly when water temperatures are rising and is diagnosed by examination of wet preparations under the high power (about 40 ×) of a microscope.

Gyrodactylus. A monogenetic fluke living on the skin of parr, to which it adheres by hooks and suckers. These parasites are up to 1 mm long and therefore easily seen under a low power microscope or even with the naked eye. They are viviparous, *ie* give birth to live young, so that infection easily spreads from fish to fish by contact.

Ichthyophthirius. This protozoan is the cause of 'white spot' disease, so called because it forms small white pustules in the skin. Adult parasites break out of the pustules and swim about for a while before encysting on the bottom of the tank or pond. After further development about 500 small infective individuals emerge from the cyst and invade any fish they make contact with. The speed with which the life cycle is completed increases with temperature, so this parasite is especially troublesome in summer.

Chilodonella and *Trichodina.* These genera are often grouped together as the '*Trichodina* complex'. They are protozoans intermediate in size between *Costia* and *Ichthyophthirius,* and they attack the skin or gills of salmonids from the fry stage onwards.

Symptoms

All the above species are ectoparasites living on the skin or gills of fish, and fish frequently show similar behavioural symptoms when infested by any one of them. The irritation brought about by skin parasites frequently causes an increase in the secretion of mucus, resulting in a blue-grey film on the fish skin. Swimming behaviour is often affected, and this most commonly takes the form of 'flashing' *ie* the fish momentarily roll onto their sides revealing their silver flanks and bellies. In some cases heavily infested fish will rub themselves against the sides of their tanks or any other hard object.

Treatment

Treatment is also similar for most ectoparasitic infestations. Formalin added to the water is a universally accepted treatment, and can be administered in one of three ways:

(1) As a dip.
    Formalin solution is made up in a container into which the fish, usually held in a small net, are dipped for a few seconds.

(2) As a bath.

Water flow through the fish tank or pond is stopped, formalin is added, and fish are left for a time before the water flow is resumed.

(3) As a flush.

Formalin is added gradually to the inlet of the fish container and allowed to flow through with the current.

In practice, dips are seldom used for formalin treatment, partly because they entail handling of fish. Because of the longer contact time and the lack of water exchange bath treatment uses less formalin than a dip or flush. Concentrations of formalin of 1:4,000 to 1:6,000 for up to one hour are recommended. However, in most systems there is a danger that fish will become short of oxygen if the water flow is stopped for long. This is made worse by the fact that formalin itself removes oxygen from solution in the water. Flush treatment is often used in raceways, but for the circulating-type tanks or ponds common in Norway, and for earth ponds, a compromise between bath and flush is normally used. The water in the container is first drawn down to half its original level or less. With the inflowing water still running the formalin is then added, either all at once in the case of small tanks or gradually with the incoming water in large ponds. Initial concentration can be up to 1:2,000 in small tanks. As the water inflow is not stopped the concentration of formalin gradually decreases as the water in the container is exchanged.

Ichthyophthirius is more difficult to remove than most ectoparasites as, for part of the life cycle, the organisms are partially protected within the skin tissues of the host fish. Some workers have obtained better results by adding about 4 g of zinc-free malachite green to each litre of formalin (Hoffman and Meyer, 1974). This stock solution is then applied to the fish at a concentration of about 1:40,000. Malachite green is also used to treat fungal infections of eggs (Chapter 4).

Some species of *Gyrodactylus* live in brackish or salt water, but those causing problems in Norwegian salmonid farms can only live in fresh water. An alternative method of control for these parasites is to flush infected tanks with water of high salinity, either pumped from the sea or produced by dissolving ordinary salt in fresh water. Bathing in 31‰ sea water or a solution of 5 kg of salt in 160 litres of water for 6–8 minutes each week or 10 days for 2–3 applications has proved effective in Norwegian experiments (Bergsjø and Vassvik, 1977).

SEA WATER

Disease organisms

Only two diseases are commonly troublesome in Norwegian sea water fish farms:

The bacterium Vibrio anguillarum. This pathogen is responsible for more financial loss than any other in the production cycle of salmonids in Norway. It occurs on wild sea fish of many species, and the bacteria are also present free in sea water. Rainbow trout, pink salmon and char can be attacked at any size or age, but Atlantic salmon are normally only vulnerable in the parr and smolt stages of development and perhaps as they approach maturity. Vibriosis in salmon therefore occurs in smolt units which pump water in from the sea and in sea units immediately after smolts are stocked out. The *Vibrio* bacterium usually enters fish through a surface wound and acts mostly on the skin, where lesions are formed. However, ulcers can extend deep into the muscles, and internal haemorrhage, kidney damage, and swollen spleens are sometimes found in dying fish. Growth of the bacterium is accelerated at higher temperature, so vibriosis is typically a disease of spring and summer.

Sea lice. These crustaceans, of the genus *Lepeophtheirus,* are common on salmonids in sea water, and the presence of a few does no harm. However in fish farms, where fish are crowded together, the numbers of sea lice occasionally build up to epidemic proportions. In Norway sea lice are most troublesome in the area of the island of Frøya, where many sea water fish farms are situated close together. The feeding activities of many lice can cause ulcers in the skin of fish. Apart from the direct mechanical damage these adversely affect the appearance of the carcass, and therefore its sale value, and may also allow entry of other pathogens such as *Vibrio*.

Treatment

Treatment of vibriosis is by addition of drugs to the food. In the later stages of infection with *Vibrio* fish frequently lose their appetites, so it is important that diagnosis should be made early and treatment started without delay. Sulphamerazine is administered at the rate of $0.2\,g/kg$ of fish/day for three days, followed by a day or two without treatment and then a further three days at $0.2\,g/kg$ of fish. Alternatively oxytetracycline is given at $50-75\,mg/kg$ of fish/day for up to 10 days. Fish should not be sold for human consumption until at least three weeks after the end of the treatment.

In the USA some success has been achieved in developing vaccines against *Vibrio* for Pacific salmon. Similar vaccines for Atlantic salmon and rainbow trout are being developed in Norway. Results so far indicate that vaccinated rainbow trout do develop a higher level of antibodies than control fish, but antibody titre is very variable and it has not yet been shown that vaccinated fish are more resistant to vibriosis under fish farm conditions. Vaccines can be given by injection, orally, or in a dip.

In floating cages treatment for sea lice is difficult, but formalin has been successfully used in a few cases. Cages can be temporarily lined with polythene sheeting, thus forming a large plastic bag containing the fish and water, into which sufficient formalin is poured to give the required concentration (about 1:5,000).

Norwegian experiments with Neguvon® have indicated that this drug can be effective against sea lice when administered orally or as a bath (Brandal and Egidius, 1977). However, Neguvon is not yet registered in Norway for use on fish for human consumption.

FISH DISEASE LEGISLATION

The Diseases of Fish Act

A number of very serious fish diseases, including viral ones, have occurred in Norway in isolated cases. To enable these diseases to be eradicated or controlled the Fish Diseases Act 1968 was introduced. The main points of the Act relevant to fish farms are:

(1) The owner or manager of a fish farm must notify a veterinarian if he suspects that he has one of the diseases covered by the Act on his farm. The notifiable diseases affecting salmonids are: whirling disease, viral haemorrhagic septicemia (VHS), furunculosis, infectious pancreatic necrosis (IPN), kidney disease, ulcer disease, ulcerative dermal necrosis (UDN), and infectious haemopoietic necrosis (IHN). In 1973 vibriosis was added to the list, but this disease is exempted from the part of the Act forbidding the sale of infected fish (section 2 below). Most of these diseases are now fortunately never found, but in 1976 a total of 61 cases of vibriosis were notified from 25 fish farms.

(2) It is prohibited to sell, give away, or release fish suspected of having any of the above diseases.

(3) Importation of live fish or fish eggs is forbidden. However, special permission from the Ministry of Agriculture can be obtained to import eggs from properly certified sources.

(4) Before a new fish farm can be established the potential farmer must have permission from the Ministry of Agriculture's Veterinary Division. In practice a farmer applies for a licence from the Department of

Fisheries, which in turn consults the Ministry of Agriculture for any veterinary objections.

(5) Veterinary officers or inspectors have power of entry to fish farms.

Inspection of farms

In practice there is little routine veterinary inspection of sea water fish farms, as there is little risk of any disease spreading from these. However, units producing smolts or fingerlings for sale are sometimes inspected as these could spread disease over a wide area. Inspectors have the power to ban sales of fish from an infected unit or even to order compulsory slaughter of stock. In the latter case financial compensation could be made by government, but this has never been necessary so far.

Companies wishing to export salmonid eggs from Norway must of course satisfy the regulations of importing countries. The Norwegian Veterinary Institute will conduct the routine tests required for such farmers, currently free of charge.

Registration of drugs

There are no restrictions on the use of chemicals freely available from an ordinary chemist's shop, *eg* formalin and malachite green. Other drugs, *eg* oxytetracycline and sulphamerazine, must be registered by the Ministry of Health for use on fish and can only be obtained with a veterinarian's prescription. A farmer who suspects his fish have a disease requiring these drugs must contact his local vet, who will telephone one of the fish food manufacturers. Both the major suppliers of fish foods in Norway produce medicated dry food pellets and medicated meal for incorporation in wet diets.

10 Marketing

Salmon and rainbow trout farms in Norway aim to produce fish as large as possible, the mean size at slaughter being about 4 kg for salmon and 2 kg for rainbow trout. As is the case for all fish species, there is a great variation in growth rate between individuals, and therefore a wide range of fish size at slaughter. For salmon the normal range in weight is 1–9 kg, and for rainbow trout 0.5–5 kg.

Salmon

Farmed salmon of this size range are very similar to the wild Atlantic salmon taken by the capture fishery, which have been prized on the European market for very many years and for which demand always exceeds supply. Consequently there has been relatively little difficulty in fitting farmed fish into the existing market outlets for this species. Even so, in the early days of salmon farming some prejudice against cultured salmon was experienced. People equated farmed fish with battery chickens and expected them to be cheaper. It is difficult to know how much this was due to a genuine belief that the farmed product would be inferior to the wild one, and how much was merely the buyers' natural desire to talk down the price if they could. However, nowadays farmed salmon are accepted by the markets as in every way equal to wild fish, and at times they even command a higher price due to being available at seasons when wild fish are not.

Rainbow trout

The rainbow trout produced in Norway have no wild counterpart on the market. European consumers know rainbow trout as the small, portion-size fish which are the products of fresh water trout farms. The member countries of the European Economic Community alone produce about 60 thousand tonnes of such fish annually, and the Norwegian output of around two thousand tonnes of large rainbow trout is too small to change the public image of the trout outside Norway itself. The costs of producing large rainbow trout are higher than those of portion-size fish, though the latter have certainly risen much in recent years. The 1976 wholesale price paid to Danish trout farmers, for example, was the equivalent of about NKr 11 per kilo. At the same time Norwegian producers received between 13 and 21 Kr/kg depending on the size of fish produced, and it is doubtful if they could have afforded to drop their price much below that and remain in business. While all trout remain equal in the eyes of the consumer, therefore, there is no way that Norwegian producers can compete successfully on foreign markets for this species.

In quality there is no doubt in the author's mind that Norwegian rainbow trout are greatly superior to the fish grown in the rest of Europe. The size, meat colour and texture, and superb flavour of the Norwegian product are much closer to the attributes of salmon than they are to portion-size rainbow trout. Norwegian rainbow trout does compete to some extent in the European market with frozen Pacific salmon, imported from the capture fisheries of Canada and elsewhere. When the market price of Pacific salmon is high, sales prospects for Norwegian trout are good. However, it must be admitted that sales promotion of Norwegian rainbow trout as a new high quality product in its own right has not been too successful.

SLAUGHTER AND PROCESSING

Norwegian farmed salmon and trout will always be expensive products which must find sales in the luxury market. It is vital, therefore, that their reputation for quality should be maintained, and a very important part of quality control is in methods of slaughter and handling of carcasses immediately prior to sale. Careless management at this stage can spoil, in a few hours, a product which has taken up to four years of husbandry to produce.

Starving

It is advisable that all fish be starved for a sufficient time for their alimentary canals to empty before they are harvested. A period of seven days without food is recommended. There are several reasons for this.

Firstly, a period of starvation tends to 'firm up' the flesh. Secondly, some fish are sold whole, *ie* with their internal organs still in place. An intestine full of bacteria and part-digested food would cause rapid deterioration of the carcass. Thirdly, even when fish are to be gutted the presence of large quantities of faeces and other intestinal contents during processing would increase the chances of bacterial contamination of carcasses.

Harvesting

Fish must be removed from their enclosures, usually floating net cages, as gently and as quickly as possible. If fish are handled roughly not only is the appearance of the carcasses impaired by skin blemishes and bruising of the meat, but subsequent deterioration of the tissues is accelerated. Speed is necessary if fish are not to die of suffocation, which affects meat quality. There is also evidence that meat quality is adversely affected if fish are stressed too much just before slaughter. It is essential that fish are not left lying about in the air, and even worse in the sun, otherwise non-reversible degenerative processes will begin.

Transport

Large fish farming companies do their own slaughtering and packing, but naturally there are strict government hygiene regulations covering this, and fairly expensive facilities are required especially if the fish are to be frozen. For most small fish farms, the salmon or trout cease to be the responsibility of the farmer after harvest. Before harvesting he makes an arrangement to sell his fish to a wholesaler, who will normally collect them from the farm either alive or freshly bled (see below) on ice. Fish leave the farm by live-hauling boat or in plastic tanks either on a boat or on the back of a truck.

There are only about 10 important wholesalers dealing in farmed salmonids in Norway, and for most of these salmon and trout form only a very small part of their business. Mostly they deal in marine fish from the capture fishery. That the facilities for processing fish were available in all coastal parts of Norway was another advantage the new fish farming industry had in this fishing nation.

Bleeding

To obtain the best possible meat quality in the carcass it is necessary to bleed fish. This improves the appearance and taste of the meat, and slows down degenerative processes. To drain properly the fish must be bled alive. The usual procedure is to stab each fish by hand with a knife just behind the gills (*Fig* 71). This severs major blood vessels. The fish are then put into tanks of cold running water (*Fig* 72) or into small floating nets (*Fig* 73) and allowed to bleed for a few minutes. Before bleeding, fish are sometimes anaesthetized by putting them into tanks through which carbon dioxide gas is bubbled, or stunned by a blow on the head. More usually, though, no anaesthetization is done. Bleeding is expensive, as the fish lose about 2% of their body weight, but it is essential in fish for the European market. Bleeding can be done on the farm before the fish leave for the packing plant, or immediately after arrival there.

Packing

After bleeding, carcasses pass onto a table in the packing plant, where they are gutted (if required) and cleaned by hand (*Fig* 74). They are then weighed and graded according to size (*Fig* 75) and sealed into the sizes of packs required by the customer. Much rainbow trout is sold frozen in plastic wrappings, but around 80% of salmon is sold fresh. This is packed between layers of flake ice in polystyrene boxes, frequently 20 kg per box (*Figs* 76 and 77). Fresh fish always commands a higher price than frozen.

Fig 71. Salmon are stabbed behind the gills with a knife to bleed them.

143

Fig 72. Rainbow trout left to drain of blood in a tank of running water.

Fig 73. Fish are cut and put into a small floating cage to bleed.

144

A/S Mowi, for example, calculates that this price difference, plus the extra costs of labour and power involved in freezing, means about Kr 5 per kilo less profit to the company if it sells its salmon frozen than if it sells fresh. Consequently, except for special orders, Mowi will only freeze fish when it is forced to harvest from its sea enclosures (Chapter 6) to reduce stocking density at a time when the market is depressed.

Fig 74. Salmon are cleaned and gutted by hand.

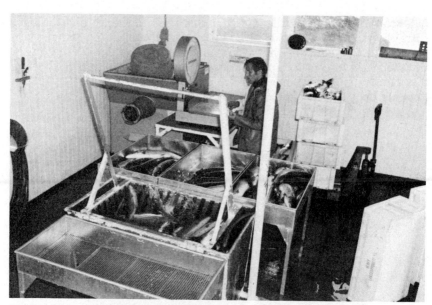

Fig 75. Salmon are weighed and graded into size groups.

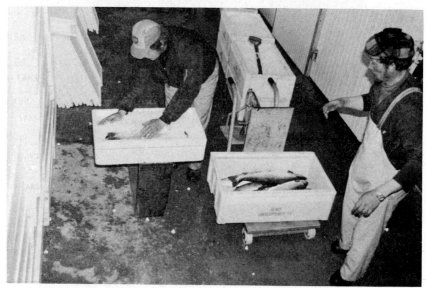

Fig 76. Salmon are weighed and packed in crushed ice.

Fig 77. Polystyrene boxes of iced salmon ready for transport.

MARKETS

A few of the large producers which do their own slaughtering and packing also handle their own sales, both for the home and export market. Sometimes these companies sell fish under their own brand name, and in this case a metal tag bearing the company's trade mark is frequently clipped onto one of the gill covers of each fish before packing. For most farms, however, sales to Norwegian and overseas markets are handled by the same wholesalers who slaughtered and packed the fish.

Over 80% of salmon, but only about 25% of rainbow trout, farmed in Norway is exported. The most important overseas customer is the EEC bloc, amongst the member nations of which West Germany and France are the biggest customers. Outside the EEC Sweden is the best customer, but other European countries, *eg* Switzerland, take significant amounts. Very little Norwegian trout or salmon is currently sold outside Europe, but attempts are being made to sell small quantities of high-value products, especially smoked salmon, on the American market.

Because it is the biggest market, EEC import regulations and sale

147

prices have a great effect on Norwegian salmonid growers and processors, both financially and in determining the form of product they produce.

Duties

Officially an import duty of 4% is payable on all Norwegian salmon imported fresh or frozen into the EEC. However, since EEC annual consumption of salmon is 40–50 thousand tonnes (of which about 10 thousand tonnes is Atlantic salmon), and its production from the fishing industries of member countries totals only about six thousand tonnes (all Atlantic salmon), demand for salmon within the Market always greatly exceeds home supply. There is therefore little need to protect the producers in member countries against foreign competition. The result is that the 4% duty has not been enforced for a number of years, and fresh or frozen Norwegian salmon enters the EEC tax free.

On the other hand, to protect its own producers the EEC levies a duty of 12% on rainbow trout entering the Community. This is strictly enforced, and is a further factor hindering the establishment of Norwegian rainbow trout on European markets.

A large proportion of the salmon eaten in the EEC is bought by the consumer smoked. Since smoked salmon commands a much higher price than fresh, Norwegians would naturally like to do the smoking themselves and export the finished product, and this is done for part of the production. However, import duties again intervene since, to protect the fish smoking industries in member countries, the EEC imposes a strictly enforced tax of 14% on salmon or trout imported ready smoked (or in other ways 'processed'). Consequently most fish enters the Community fresh or frozen and is processed in the country in which it will be consumed.

No taxes are imposed on Norwegian salmon or trout entering Sweden.

PRICES

Food fish

For food fish, *ie* large salmon and rainbow trout, prices fluctuate according to the state of the market. Since most salmon is exported, its price is influenced by the balance of supply and demand in Europe as a whole. In recent years there has always been a shortage of salmon, and prices have been high. As mentioned above, price of rainbow trout is influenced by the state of the European market not only for trout, but also for Pacific salmon. However, as most Norwegian rainbow trout is sold on the home market, the price the farmer receives is much more a domestic matter than that of salmon.

There is now some co-operation between producers and buyers in agreeing prices in Norway. Representatives of the wholesalers annually meet the board of the Norwegian Fish Farmers' Association (see below) to decide on fair prices, taking into account overseas price levels and demand. The prices arrived at are only guidelines and have no legal validity. They are not always adhered to and there are always local variations in price, especially for salmon. However, the fact that producers and buyers are prepared to discuss each others' point of view and seek prices reasonable to both sides has gone some way towards bringing stability to the industry.

The price arrived at for each actual sale will take into account the degree of flesh pigmentation and the general condition of fish, but the main criterion for pricing is size. The larger the fish the higher the price they will fetch per kilo on the market. Prices vary from year to year, but 1976 averages are given in *Table* 7. These figures are used in the budget calculations in Chapter 11.

Table 7. Average 1976 wholesale prices of Norwegian farmed salmon and rainbow trout.

Size of fish	Price per kilo in Norwegian kroner	
	Salmon	Rainbow trout
Up to 1 kg	—	13
1–2 kg	20–25	15
2–3 kg	25–30	17
3–4 kg	30–40	19.60
4–5 kg	40–45	20.60
5– kg	45–50	—

Smolts and fingerlings

The prices of salmon smolts and rainbow trout fingerlings ready for transfer to the sea are much more of an internal Norwegian matter than those of food fish, and can therefore be regulated more exactly. Again, fair prices are set by agreement following discussion between representatives of producers and buyers (who, in this case, are themselves fish farmers) at meetings of the Norwegian Fish Farmers' Association. Though these prices are not legally binding they are fairly well adhered to.

Up to and including 1976, rainbow trout fingerlings were sold by weight but smolts by number, though large smolts always commanded a

149

price premium over small ones. 1976 prices were NKr 5.75 each for smolts and Kr 22 per kilo for rainbow trout fingerlings. From 1977, however, a more complicated pricing system which takes size of fish more into account will be used. An attempt is also being made to standardize prices of eggs and salmon parr. *Table* 8 shows recommended 1977 prices.

Table 8. Recommended 1977 prices for young salmon and rainbow trout in Norway.

Product	Price in Norwegian kroner
(1) Atlantic salmon	
Eggs (newly fertilized):	300 per litre
Eggs (eyed):	600–800 per litre, or 100–125 per thousand eggs
Parr, 5–8 g:	0.50 each, or 0.15 per cm
Smolts, under 20 g:	3 each
Smolts, 20–30 g:	5 each
Smolts, 30–35 g:	6.50 each
Smolts, over 35 g:	7 each
(2) Rainbow trout	
Eyed eggs:	40–80 per thousand
Fingerlings, 70 g:	1.50–1.55 each
Fingerlings, 100 g:	2.20 each
Fingerlings, 120 g:	2.40 each

FISH FARMERS' ORGANIZATIONS

In the early days the marketing of farmed fish was disorganized and sometimes chaotic. One constraint on development of the industry was uncertainty over prices; no one knew when he planted out his young fish how much he could expect to get for the crop 18 months or two years later. One of the disadvantages of the Norwegian method of fish culture is that there is always a deadline by which time the crop must be harvested, *ie* before fish become fully sexually mature. This can lead to a seasonal glut of fish. Before small producers had any organization they were therefore prey to disastrous drops in prices at times of high availability. This culminated in the mid sixties in 'panic selling' of rainbow trout at ridiculously low prices, an experience which frightened many producers out of the business.

The Norwegian Trout Sales Organization

As a result of these marketing difficulties a co-operative organization was set up in 1965. The Norwegian Trout Sales Organization buys rainbow

150

trout from its member producers and sells to wholesalers within Norway. It is able to provide loans and guarantee a minimum price to farmers, thus bringing a much greater degree of financial security to its members. The organization now represents over 50% of Norway's rainbow trout farmers.

The Norwegian Meat Marketing Board

This co-operative organization has for many years regulated the production, slaughter, distribution, import and export of meat in Norway. In 1974 it became involved in the fish farming industry, mostly dealing with salmon. The Board buys smolts or fingerlings in bulk and distributes them to its members. It can also provide credit or loans of up to 50% to farmers for the purchase of smolts. When the crop is ready for harvest the Board organizes sales to wholesalers. Members, who are individually only small producers, therefore have the advantage of both buying and selling their fish through a larger organization which is better able to protect their interests. Although the Meat Marketing Board currently handles only a fairly small percentage of salmon farmed in Norway, its membership and importance in the industry are likely to increase.

The Norwegian Fish Farmers' Association

The Association was established in 1970 with the following major aims:

(*1*) To provide fish farmers with a trade union to represent their interests to government and buyers. It now claims around 70% of the country's fish farmers as voluntary, paying members. This total includes almost all the large producers, so the members would account for considerably more than 70% of the annual output of fish. Some of the members also belong to the Norwegian Trout Sales Organization, and the Meat Marketing Board is itself an active member of the Fish Farmers' Association.

(*2*) To help organize sales and stabilize prices by negotiating price guidelines recognized as fair by both producers and buyers (see above). There is a possibility that the Association may in the future itself take part in the actual marketing of salmon produced by its members, in much the same way as the Trout Sales Organization already does for rainbow trout.

(*3*) To promote sales of farmed salmon and trout by disseminating information and advertising literature about Norwegian products both inside the country and abroad.

(*4*) To provide members with up-to-date information on fish farming techniques and markets. Since 1976 the Association has published its own magazine for Norwegian fish farmers. This aims to present information on new developments in salmonid culture. Articles are contributed by scientists, fish farmers, economists *etc.* The Association also organizes package tours to successful fish farming operations in Norway and elsewhere in Europe.

11 Economics

It is very difficult to generalize about the financial budgets of Norwegian salmon and trout farms. Every unit will be different according to its type, location, size, management *etc*, and each aspiring fish farmer must make his own detailed calculations for his particular site and intentions. The aim of this chapter is primarily to allow some comparison of the potential profitability of farming rainbow trout in the two ways practised in Norway (Chapter 2), and of salmon production. Only secondarily is it intended to give an indication of the actual cash rewards which can be made in salmonid farming. Very little economic analysis of operating Norwegian fish farms has been published, so in this chapter it is necessary to start from basic principles.

To set down any figures at all it is necessary to put arbitrary limits on some of the variables, and to make assumptions to simplify the calculations. The basic assumptions made here are:

(1) Type of production
Only that part of the production cycle in which smolts or fingerlings are grown-on to harvest in the sea is considered. It is assumed that the young fish are bought from specialist suppliers; those companies which produce their own smolts or fingerlings would therefore expect to make savings on this part of the budget.

(2) Unit construction
Fish are grown in the most common Norwegian way, *ie* in floating net cages moored singly and serviced by a small boat. Fixed enclosures are not considered here. It is assumed that the farmer owns the land from which he operates, that both a building suitable for storage of food and equipment and a quay are available, and that a track good enough for delivery of food and transport of slaughtered fish is present.

(3) Size of unit
The size of unit considered is that which could reasonably be run for

most of the year by one man, who is also the owner, as a full-time job. Assistance would be needed to cover holidays, sickness, and for limited periods of the year to help with heavy jobs such as changing nets and harvesting. Under these circumstances an annual production of 20 metric tons is not unreasonable.

(4) Sale of fish

Fish are sold whole off the farm at standard wholesale price.

(5) Food

It is assumed that commercially produced dry, pelleted food is used, and is delivered to the fish by hand.

Other assumptions will be discussed as they arise in the calculations.

In all calculations 1976 prices in Norwegian kroner are used (at the time of writing US$1=approx. NKr5.3, and £1 sterling=approx. NKr9.1). Prices will obviously change through inflation as time passes but, if figures are considered merely as numbers, the relative costs and rewards may still be valid.

RAINBOW TROUT

Production of rainbow trout in one year

This is the simplest production cycle, and will be considered first.

Investment. (1) Equipment needed to start production

(a) *Floating net cages.* Many types of these are available at a variety of prices, but for the purposes of these calculations it is assumed that the popular 'Tess' 300 cubic metre cages marketed by T Skretting A/S of Stavanger are used. Home-made flotation systems could be cheaper.

The number of cages needed to produce 20 tonnes of fish at harvest depends on the stocking density used. If the reasonably low density of 10kg/m^3 is assumed, each 300m^3 cage will hold 3 tonnes of fish, and to produce 20 tonnes: $20 \div 3 = 6.67$, *ie* 7 cages, would be needed.

Cages are bought complete with net bags, but as it is necessary to change nets for cleaning approximately twice a year spare bags are needed. It is assumed that one is bought for each cage.

Cages require moorings, the amount needed depending on the location, but Kr 1,000 per net is a reasonable average cost.

(b) *A small boat* is required for feeding fish and generally working the nets. A suitable model complete with a small outboard engine can be obtained for Kr 8,000.

(2) Annual running costs

(a) *Fish.* Fingerlings are bought in autumn at a mean weight of 70 g. It is reasonable to assume these will reach a mean weight of 1.5 kg by the following autumn, when they are slaughtered. Losses in the meantime are variable, but an allowance of 25% for this is generous.

Therefore, to produce 20 tonnes of fish at a mean weight of 1.5 kg there must be $\dfrac{20,000}{1.5} = 13,333$ fish left.

To get this with 25% loss $\dfrac{13,333}{3} \times 4 = 17,777$ fingerlings must be stocked out.

Rainbow trout fingerlings are sold by weight, and at a mean weight of 70 g this would be $\dfrac{17,777 \times 70}{1000} = 1,244$ kg, which at Kr 22 per kilo (Chapter 10) would cost Kr27,377.

Costs for delivery of young fish vary a little according to the distance and method of transportation involved. An average figure for both trout fingerlings and salmon smolts is 50 øre each. In this example, then, delivery charges would be $17,777 \times 0.5 = $ Kr8,889.

(b) *Food.* Cost of food varies according to its chemical composition and delivery distance, but a good quality high calorie ('salmon') food costs an average of about Kr3 per kilo delivered.

With a slaughter weight of 20 tonnes the fish will have gained $20,000 - 1,244$ (the start weight) $= 18,756$ kg.

Assuming an overall food conversion of 2:1 this will require $18,756 \times 2 = 37,512$ kg of food, at a cost of $37,512 \times 3 = $ Kr112,536.

(c) *Impregnation of nets.* Nets normally require cleaning about twice a year, and re-impregnation with an anti-fouling preparation either once or twice per year. The cost of re-impregnation varies according to whether the farmer does it himself or sends his nets away to be treated, and the preparation he uses. If he does the job himself with commercially made anti-foulant a cost of Kr200 per net is reasonable, and taking the pessimistic view that this must be done twice per year the annual cost will be Kr400 per net, *ie* a total of Kr2,800 per year in this example.

(d) *Labour.* Leaving aside the farmer's own labour, extra help will be needed for holidays and work requiring more than one pair of hands. Allowing three weeks holiday away from the unit, one week for sickness, and four weeks help at net changing and harvest, a cost of around Kr12,000 might be incurred, inclusive of employment taxes.

155

Annual budget. (1) Investment
Total investment for equipment needed to start production is:

7 cages at Kr 8,000	....	Kr 56,000
7 spare nets at Kr 2,500	....	Kr 17,500
Moorings	....	Kr 7,000
Boat + motor	....	Kr 8,000
Total	....	Kr 88,500

For the purposes of these budget calculations a 5-year depreciation time is assumed on all equipment. Annual depreciation cost is therefore Kr 17,700.

Running costs:

Fingerlings	....	Kr 27,377
Delivery	....	Kr 8,889
Food	....	Kr 112,536
Net impregnation	....	Kr 2,800
Extra labour	....	Kr 12,000
Total	....	Kr 163,602

Interest: for the purposes of this calculation it is assumed that half the initial cost of equipment and annual running expenses is borrowed. The usual cost of borrowing money from a bank in Norway is currently 8%, but loans guaranteed by the District Development Fund cost only $6\frac{1}{2}\%$. Using the higher figure,

$$\text{Annual cost of interest} = \frac{88,500 + 163,602}{2} \times \frac{8}{100} = \text{Kr} 10,084.$$

Total annual costs (allowing 10% for miscellaneous expenses not included in the calculations, *eg* insurance, electricity, rent of land):

Depreciation	....	Kr 17,700
Interest	....	Kr 10,084
Running costs	....	Kr 163,602
		Kr 191,386
+ 10%	....	Kr 19,139
Total	....	Kr 210,525

(2) Income from the sale of 20 tonnes of rainbow trout at Kr 15 per kilo (average 1976 price for 1.5 kg fish, Chapter 10) = 20,000 × 15 = Kr 300,000.

156

(*3*) *Annual balance* of income over expenditure left to cover the farmer's own wages and profits is 300,000−210,525 = Kr89,475.

Production of rainbow trout in 18 months.

This is a more complex production cycle, as two year-classes of fish must be held on the farm at the same time.

Investment. (1) Equipment required in the first year

If the production target is again 20 tonnes per year, at slaughter the same number of cages as before is required for harvest-ready fish, *ie* seven cages.

Slaughter is in autumn 18 months after stocking. Assuming the fish will double their weight in the last six months, after one year of operations there will be only 10 tonnes of fish. Therefore only four cages are needed to hold these fish for the first year.

(*NB* The mean weight of the fish after one year will not be quite as high as in the one-year production cycle described above. This is because those fish spent their year in the sea from autumn to autumn, and therefore had their summer season of fast growth shortly before slaughter. In the present case the first year is from spring to spring, so that the warm season comes when the fish are smaller, and individual weight gain is therefore less.)

Equipment costs for the first year, calculated on the same basis as before, are therefore:

4 complete cages	Kr 32,000
4 spare nets	Kr 10,000
Moorings	Kr 4,000
Boat + motor	Kr 8,000
Total	Kr 54,000

(2) Equipment required in the second year

The fish carried over from the previous year are only kept for six months before slaughter. Nevertheless they require seven cages by the time they are ready for harvest at 20 tonnes total weight.

To give annual production, new fingerlings must be brought into the farm in spring to provide fish for harvest the following year. These will be in the same numbers as before, and will therefore require four cages.

The total requirement for cages in the second year is therefore 11, so seven new ones must be bought. In addition moorings for new cages, and more spare nets, are needed.

157

Consequently, second year equipment costs are:

7 complete cages	....	Kr 56,000
7 spare nets	....	Kr 17,500
Moorings	....	Kr 7,000
Total	....	Kr 80,500

(3) Running costs in the first year

(a) *Fish.* A reasonable average weight after 18 months would be 2.5 kg. Therefore, for 20 tonnes of production there must be 8,000 fish left at harvest. Allowing 25% for losses, this means starting with 10,667 fingerlings which, at a mean weight of 70 g, represents 747 kg costing (at Kr 22/kg) Kr 16,428.

Delivery cost at 50 øre each = Kr 5,334.

(b) *Food.* In the first year the fish reach a total weight of 10 tonnes, *ie* a gain of 10,000−747 = 9,253 kg.

At a 2:1 conversion this requires 18,506 kg of food at Kr 3/kg = Kr 55,518.

(c) *Net impregnation* at Kr 400 per net = Kr 1,600.

(d) *Labour.* Assuming the same extra labour is required as above, the cost will again be Kr 12,000. In practice it would be less, as fewer nets are used during the first year of operation, and no harvesting is done.

(4) Running costs in the second year

(a) *Fish.* The same amount of fingerlings are needed as the previous year, at a cost of Kr 16,428 plus Kr 5,334 for delivery.

(b) *Food.* The new, young fish will need the same food as those the previous year, *ie* Kr 55,518.

The older fish will double their weight, *ie* gain 10 tonnes, requiring 20 tonnes of food costing Kr 60,000.

Therefore total food cost in the second year is 55,518 + 60,000 = Kr 115,518.

(c) *Impregnation of nets.* There are now 11 nets, but seven of these containing older fish will only be used for half the year, so it can be assumed they only need re-impregnating once. Impregnation costs for the year are therefore:

4 × Kr 400	....	Kr 1,600
7 × Kr 200	....	Kr 1,400
Total	....	Kr 3,000

(*d*) *Labour*. It will again be assumed that the same extra labour is required as before. In fact it will be more this year than last as there are now more cages, and fish must be harvested for the first time. Allowance for labour = Kr 12,000.

Two-year budget. (*1*) *The total investment in the first two years is*
Equipment:

Year 1	Kr 54,000
Year 2	Kr 80,500
Total	Kr 134,500

Allowing a 5-year depreciation time, the annual depreciation cost is Kr 26,900.

Running costs: Year 1:

Fingerlings	Kr 16,428
Delivery	Kr 5,334
Food	Kr 55,518
Net impregnation	Kr 1,600
Labour	Kr 12,000
First year total	Kr 90,880

Year 2:

Fingerlings	Kr 16,428
Delivery	Kr 5,334
Food	Kr 115,518
Net impregnation	Kr 3,000
Labour	Kr 12,000
Second year total	Kr 152,280

Total running costs over the first two years = 90,880 + 152,280 = Kr 243,160.

Interest on borrowed capital:

$$\text{Year 1:} \quad \frac{54,000 + 90,880}{2} \times \frac{8}{100} = \text{Kr5,795.}$$

$$\text{Year 2:} \quad \frac{134,500 + 243,160}{2} \times \frac{8}{100} = \text{Kr15,106.}$$

Total interest for the first two years = Kr 20,901.

Total costs over the first two years are therefore:

Depreciation, 2 × 26,900	Kr	53,800
Running costs	Kr	243,160
Interest	Kr	20,901
	Kr	317,861
+ 10%	Kr	31,786
Total	Kr	349,647

(2) *An income* from sale of fish is obtained half way through the second year. For 20 tonnes of an average weight of 2.5 kg this will be 20,000 × Kr 17 (average 1976 price for fish of this size, Chapter 10) = Kr 340,000.

(3) *Balance* of income over expenditure for the first two years is therefore 340,000–349,647, a negative balance of Kr 9,647. The farm in this example does not quite break even after 18 months.

Annual budget in subsequent years

From the second year of operation onwards the farm produces the same annual income for a constant annual investment.

(1) *Annual investment:*

Depreciation	Kr	26,900
Running costs	Kr	152,280
Interest	Kr	11,471
	Kr	190,651
+ 10%	Kr	19,065
Total	Kr	209,716

(2) *Annual income* = Kr 340,000.

(3) *Annual balance* of income over expenditure = 340,000–209,716 = Kr 130,284.

Comparison of the two systems for producing rainbow trout

To a man wishing to start farming rainbow trout, the greatest advantage of the one-year cycle method is that an income from sale of fish is obtained after only one year. In the two-year cycle it is 18 months before any return at all is obtained and, as the above example shows, it may take until the second crop is harvested, *ie* $2\frac{1}{2}$ years after starting operations, before any profit is made to pay wages to the farmer himself.

Once the 18-month cycle is in operation it may give a higher return per tonne of fish produced, as there is a price premium on larger fish. However, to produce the same tonnage of fish considerably more equipment is required in the longer cycle, *eg* in the above example to produce 20 tonnes 11 cages are required for six months of the year, as compared to seven in the one-year cycle. This must mean more work. If the farmer felt able to run 11 cages all year round, and used them to grow rainbow trout by the one-year method, at three tonnes per cage this could produce an annual 33 tonnes of fish worth Kr495,000. For this his annual investment calculated on the same basis as above would be:

Equipment:

11 complete cages	Kr	88,000
11 spare nets	Kr	27,500
Moorings	Kr	11,000
Boat + motor	Kr	8,000
Total	Kr	134,500

Depreciation over five years = Kr26,900 per year.
Annual running costs:

Fingerlings	Kr	45,173
Delivery	Kr	14,667
Food	Kr	198,000
Impregnation	Kr	4,400
Labour	Kr	12,000
Total	Kr	274,240

Total annual investment:

Depreciation	Kr	26,900
Running costs	Kr	274,240
Interest	Kr	16,349
	Kr	317,489
+ 10%	Kr	31,748
Total	Kr	349,237

161

giving a positive annual balance of income over expenditure of 495,000−349,237=Kr 145,763.

There is little doubt that there are economic advantages in the one-year (sea water phase) cycle for rainbow trout. Many rainbow trout farmers are in fact turning over to this method of production, but some limitation is imposed by a shortage of fingerlings big enough to be transferred to the sea by the autumn of their first year of life.

SALMON

Two-year cycle

The production of salmon normally takes a full two years in the sea. Most of the growth occurs in the second year. Salmon can be expected to average about 1 kg at the end of the first year and 4 kg at harvest.

Investment (1) Equipment required in the first year.

If the production target is the same as in the rainbow trout examples, *ie* 20 tonnes per year, and the same stocking density is used, the fish at harvest will require seven cages. However, as the salmon will reach only about one quarter of their final size by the end of their first year in the sea only five tonnes must be held at the end of year one, *ie* only two cages are needed.

Equipment costs for the first year are therefore:

2 complete cages	Kr 16,000
2 spare nets	Kr 5,000
Moorings	Kr 2,000
Boat + motor	Kr 8,000
Total	Kr 31,000

(2) Equipment required in the second year

For annual production, new smolts are needed this year. They will again require two cages. An additional seven cages are needed to hold the older fish up to harvest.

Second year equipment costs are therefore:

7 complete cages	Kr 56,000
7 spare nets	Kr 17,500
Moorings	Kr 7,000
Total	Kr 80,500

(3) Running costs in the first year

(a) Fish. If fish average 4 kg at harvest, to get 20 tonnes 20,000÷4 = 5,000 fish must survive.

Losses of salmon are frequently a little higher than those of rainbow trout. In this example $33\frac{1}{3}\%$ is allowed, so to be left with 5,000 fish at slaughter 7,500 smolts must be stocked. Smolts are sold by number, the 1976 standard price being Kr5.75 each (Chapter 10). Therefore the cost of smolts is Kr43,125.

Cost of delivery = 7,500 × 0.50 = Kr3,750.

(b) Food. At the end of the first year there are five tonnes of fish. Smolts average only about 35 g in weight, so the fish have grown by

$$5,000 - \frac{7,500 \times 35}{1,000} = 4,738 \text{kg}$$

Assuming the same food is used as in the rainbow trout examples, and the same 2:1 conversion is obtained, the cost of food will be 4,738 × 2 × 3 = Kr28,428.

(c) Net impregnation at Kr400/net = Kr800.

(d) Labour. The same allowance is made, *ie* Kr12,000.

(4) Running costs in the second year

(a) Fish. The same number of smolts will be required as last year, at a cost of Kr43,125, plus Kr3,750 for delivery.

(b) Food. New smolts require the same amount of food as those last year. Cost = Kr28,428.

Older fish will increase in weight by 15 tonnes in the course of the second year. They will therefore consume 30 tonnes of food at a cost of Kr90,000.

Total food cost for year 2 = Kr118,428.

(c) Net impregnation at Kr400/net = Kr3,600.

(d) Allowance for extra labour = Kr12,000.

Two-year budget (1) Total investment in the first two years is:
Equipment:

Year 1	Kr 31,000
Year 2	Kr 80,500
Total	Kr 111,500

With a 5-year depreciation time the annual cost is Kr22,300.

Running costs: Year 1:

```
Smolts ...................... Kr   43,125
Delivery  ................... Kr    3,750
Food  ...................... Kr   28,428
Impregnation  ............... Kr      800
Labour   ................... Kr   12,000
                                 _____
First year total ............... Kr   88,103
                                 _____
```

Year 2:
```
Smolts ...................... Kr   43,125
Delivery  ................... Kr    3,750
Food  ...................... Kr  118,428
Impregnation  ............... Kr    3,600
Labour   ................... Kr   12,000
                                 _____
Second year total  ............ Kr  180,903
                                 _____
```

Total running expenses over the first two years = Kr 269,006.

Interest on borrowed capital:

$$\text{Year 1:} \quad \frac{31,000 + 88,103}{2} \times \frac{8}{100} = \text{Kr } 4,764.$$

$$\text{Year 2:} \quad \frac{111,500 + 269,006}{2} \times \frac{8}{100} = \text{Kr} 15,220.$$

Total interest for the first two years = Kr 19,984.

Total costs over the first two years are therefore:
```
Depreciation, 2 × 22,300  ........ Kr   44,600
Running costs  ............... Kr  269,006
Interest   .................... Kr   19,984
                                  _____
                                  Kr 333,590
+ 10% ...................... Kr   33,359
                                  _____
Total   ..................... Kr  366,949
                                  _____
```

(2) An income from sale of fish is obtained at the end of the second year. The price to be expected for fish averaging 4 kg is Kr 30–40 per kilo (Chapter 10). Assuming they fetch Kr 35/kg, 20 tonnes will produce an

income of Kr700,000.
(3) *Balance* of income over expenditure for the first two years is
700,000–366,949 = Kr333,051.

Annual budget in subsequent years
Again, from the second year of operation onwards the farm produces the
same annual income for a constant annual investment.

(1) *Annual investment:*

Depreciation	Kr	22,300
Running costs	Kr	180,903
Interest	Kr	15,220
	Kr	218,423
+ 10%	Kr	21,842
Total	Kr	240,265

(2) *Annual income* = Kr700,000.

(3) *Annual balance* of income over expenditure = 700,000–240,265
= Kr459,735.

COMPARISON OF SALMON AND RAINBOW TROUT PRODUCTION

At present, the potential profits of salmon farming are considerably
greater than those of rainbow trout farming, whichever production cycle
is used for trout. The reasons for this are:

(1) The high sale price of salmon. Salmon can fetch twice the price of
rainbow trout of the same size (Chapter 10), but production costs for the
two species are quite similar when the same cage-culture methods are
used.

(2) Because of their later maturity, salmon can be grown larger than
rainbow trout. This further enhances the price differential between the two
species at harvest, as the per-kilo value of both species is higher for larger
fish.

Technically, salmon production is more strictly comparable with the
traditional 18-month system of rainbow trout culture. Although the
rainbow trout are grown in the sea for only 18 months, from spring one
year to autumn the next, this is really a two-year cycle as some nets must

M

remain empty until new fingerlings are available to begin a new cycle the following spring. Salmon, however, can be left in the sea for a full two years, and in the last six months they will double their weight. This must be a more rational use of the time and facilities of the culturist and his farm.

On the other hand, rainbow trout are generally easier to culture than salmon. Salmon smolts are more easily damaged than trout fingerlings, losses of salmon tend to be higher, and all through life salmon are more demanding in their food requirements than rainbow trout. For these reasons beginners in salmonid farming are frequently advised to start with rainbow trout and, after a year or two of on-the-job experience, to turn over gradually to salmon.

NOTES ON BUDGETS

Food

In the above examples, expenditure for rainbow trout food could be reduced by about 15% if 'trout' instead of 'salmon' food was used. However, both species do grow better on the high calorie/high protein salmon foods, and the reduced average size of fish at harvest (with consequent need to stock more fingerlings to achieve the target production figure) would to a large extent offset any savings in food costs. If wet food was used, the extra labour required for food preparation would greatly reduce the production attainable per man-year.

Capital

It is possible to borrow money to cover part of the costs of equipment and running expenses, but extremely difficult to get loans to cover the owner's own wages until his first crop is ready. In practice, most Norwegian salmonid farmers start on a part-time basis, maintaining sufficient income from commercial fishing or land farming to cover their living expenses. Larger companies have been started by men who have already made sufficient capital in other fields to obviate the need to borrow much money. Frequently these are ex-trawlermen, and some retain an interest in trawling to supply their salmonid farms with industrial fish for food. Examples of this are the Grøntvedt brothers at Hitra and Mr Torrissen and his brothers near Bodø. Unlike some other countries, eg the United Kingdom, very few Norwegian fish farms have been financed by very large companies active in unrelated fields but wishing to diversify their interests. However, one which has is A/S Mowi, which is partly owned by Norsk Hydro A/S, Norway's biggest company with interests in oil, chemicals and many other things.

Labour

In the budgets, the assumption was made that most of the work was done by the owner of the farm himself, with hired labour available when necessary. In many ways the ideal size of farm is one owned and run by two men, who could easily aim to produce annually twice the 20 tonnes of fish assumed above. Where there are two worker/owners there is no necessity to hire any extra labour, so this part of the expenditure is saved. Furthermore for most of the year, when the most arduous job is feeding, the presence of only one of the men is required if dry food is used. The author knows one farm in Norway, producing about 100 tonnes of rainbow trout annually by the one-year method, in which the two owners each work only in alternate weeks for most of the year.

For larger companies, where it is necessary to hire labour, the difficulties of showing sufficient profit to give a satisfactory return on investment are greater. Nevertheless at current market prices, especially for salmon, there is no doubt that fish farming can be an extremely profitable business, and many Norwegian salmon farmers will privately admit to making annual profits of well over 100% on investment. However, the high risk nature of the industry both biologically and in possible drastic fluctuations of sale price must be weighed against potential returns.

12 The Future

CONTINUING TRENDS

There are perhaps three main trends apparent in Norwegian salmon and trout farming over the past few years. These are:

(*1*) Growth in numbers of farms and in total annual fish production.

(*2*) Shift of production from rainbow trout to salmon.

(*3*) Increased use of dry instead of wet foods for salmon and trout in sea water.

Trends *1* and *2* are closely tied to the demand of foreign markets, especially the EEC. As mentioned in Chapter 10, there is a considerable shortfall in the supply of Atlantic salmon to the EEC market by its own commercial fishermen. Since January 1976 international agreement has resulted in restrictions on fishing for salmon in the waters around Greenland and in the open sea of the North Atlantic. This has opened an even greater gap between supply and demand though the EEC's greatest salmon fishing nation, Denmark, seems reluctant to comply with the new restrictions. Norway's own capture fishery for salmon has also been hit by the regulations, to the extent of around 420 tonnes per year, resulting in a fall in the amount of wild salmon available for export. This must further enhance the opportunities for Norway's salmon farmers to expand their production to take advantage of the current European shortage of this species, and also serve to keep market prices at a profitably high level.

Future production

There are always problems in predicting future levels of production, but at the time of writing (early 1977) the likely Norwegian production of farmed salmon in 1977 and 1978 can be predicted with a fairly good degree of accuracy since the approximate numbers of smolts stocked in 1975 and 1976 are known. As a starting point, in 1974 around 800 thousand smolts were stocked. These gave a (declared) harvest of about 1,850 tonnes in 1976. Allowing one third for losses, this would make the average weight of fish at harvest

$$\frac{1,850,000}{\dfrac{800,000 \times 2}{3}} = 3.47\text{kg}$$

(This average is not quite as high as the 4 kg assumed in the calculations in Chapter 11, because not all fish are left in the sea for a full two years before harvest).

In 1975, around 1.2 million smolts were stocked. Applying the same principles as above, these should give a production at harvest in 1977 of approximately

$$\frac{1,200,000}{3} \times 2 \times 3.47\text{kg} = 2,776 \text{ tonnes.}$$

Similarly, in 1976 1.5 million smolts were stocked, giving an estimated

$$\frac{1,500,000}{3} \times 2 \times 3.47\text{kg} = 3,470 \text{ tonnes}$$

production for 1978.

Actual and projected production figures for salmon and rainbow trout are shown in *Table* 9 for the years 1971–1978.

Salmon production is clearly in a period of rapid expansion, the only limitation on which at present is the supply of smolts. Obviously such a rapid expansion cannot continue indefinitely. Once the European production fills the demand prices must stabilize or fall. When this will happen is difficult to predict, as it depends not only on the fate of the capture fishery, but also on the rate of development of salmon farming in other countries. The west coast of Scotland, for example, has a small Atlantic salmon farming industry, and next to Norway this country has the best natural conditions of sheltered sites and suitable water temperatures for this industry. The current Scottish production is small, and compares with that of Norway in 1972 or 1973. However, if Scotland's industry develops as fast in the next five years as Norway's has in the last five, the whole picture of European supply and demand for salmon could change drastically. Norway might then have to face EEC tariff barriers imposed to protect Scottish member producers. In the meantime it is the aim of Norwegian fish farmers' organizations to try to slow the rate of expansion in output to allow it to reach a balance with demand rather than undergoing the 'boom and bust' which has happened to so many new industries. There is also a need for more organization in marketing of salmon both at home and abroad, and to spread harvest over a longer period of the year.

It can be seen from *Table* 9 that no rise in rainbow trout production is expected in the next few years. This is because most trout find outlets in home sales, which are obviously limited in a country of only four million people. Significant expansion in rainbow trout production would have as a pre-requisite a successful sales drive on overseas markets to promote large, red-fleshed trout as a new, high quality product in its own right. The recognition by the EEC that Norwegian rainbow trout is not comparable with portion-size fish and does not compete with it, resulting in abolition of the import duty, would also be a great help.

Table 9. Approximate actual and projected production of farmed rainbow trout and salmon in Norway. (Figures up to 1976 by courtesy of the Norwegian Fish Farmers' Association.)

Year	Production in metric tons	
	Rainbow trout	Salmon
1971	500	150
1972	950	200
1973	1,300	250
1974	2,200	800
1975	1,800	950
1976	1,800	1,850
1977 (projected)	1,800	2,776
1978 (projected)	1,800	3,470

Increasing use of dry food

The trend towards replacement of wet food by dry for sea water production is expected to continue, reducing the work load on fish farms and making a higher production possible per man-year.

At present, some producers find that growth of salmon and trout is not as good during periods of low water temperature on dry food as on wet. Winter mortality of rainbow trout can also be higher on dry food. The reasons for this are not definitely known, but osmoregulatory difficulties have been implicated. Food acceptability may also play a part. It could be that the fish become too sluggish to catch the sinking pellets, or that the prevailing low light intensity during the Norwegian winter makes it more difficult for fish to see the dark pellets than the lighter-coloured wet food mixture. Finally, it has been suggested that the fat composition of diets is responsible. Generally, the fats present in wet diets have a lower melting point than those in dry foods, and the proportions of certain fatty acids present are also different. Food manufacturers have carried out experiments which showed that growth of salmon and trout can be just as good on dry as wet food (*eg* Hildingstam, 1976). However, it is clear that the

170

experience of many farmers does not bear this out, and there would be some benefit in independent trials being conducted, preferably in the north of Norway where water temperatures are lowest and most problems of this type occur. If this problem could be solved the use of dry foods would probably be adopted by many more Norwegian salmonid farms during the next few years.

PROMISING RESEARCH

The development of salmon and trout farming in Norway has been pushed ahead largely by intelligent guesswork tested by trial-and-error, *ie* by applied research, carried out by the farmers themselves. This is an excellent way for an industry to begin but, once workable systems have been developed and the law of diminishing returns applies to innovation, the pace of advance slows down and most producers tend to settle into the safe established practices. Also, the costs of many types of research necessary to advance the industry further are so high that only the government or very large companies can afford to indulge in them. In Norway there are so few large companies involved in fish farming that virtually all formal research is done by government. The main departments involved are listed in the Appendix, together with notes on their activities.

Selective breeding

In the historical development of terrestrial farm animal production, selective breeding to produce strains giving higher yields of the desired quality of product played a very important part, and this selection still continues today. On the other hand for salmonids complete control of the life cycle, which is an essential pre-requisite for selective breeding, has only relatively recently become possible. Some people are still using wild fish as their brood stock, and even where stocks have been kept in captivity for many generations they have changed little from the wild populations from which their ancestors came. Wild animals are not adapted to life in captivity, and there is great potential for increasing yields by breeding fish which are more productive under the artificial conditions on fish farms.

Breeding goals
    Before selective breeding can begin it is important to define carefully the traits which are important, and how it is desired to change them, *ie* to

171

define the breeding goal. The traits which scientists and farmers feel are most important for salmon and trout farmed in the Norwegian way are:

(1) *Rapid growth.* Each year salmon brood stock are collected from many different rivers (strains) and their offspring are tested for rate of growth under fish farm conditions, both in the fresh and sea water stages of life. It has been found that different strains vary greatly in their rate of growth to marketable size, fish of the best strain so far tested reaching well over twice the mean weight of the poorest by harvest time. The results of one such experiment are shown in *Table* 10. Selection can therefore start with the fastest growing wild strains available. Abroad, some success has already been reported in producing faster growing strains of rainbow trout (*eg* Donaldson and Olson, 1957). Growth rate also influences the age at smoltification. Strains of salmon which grow faster during the early, fresh water stage of their lives can be expected to produce a higher percentage of one-year-old smolts.

Table 10. Ranking of salmon strains for growth to three years of age (from Gjedrem, 1976b).

Place of origin (strain)	Mean weight at 3yr (kg)	Strain	Weight (kg)
Jordalsgrenda	5.1	Målselva	4.5
Namsen	4.9	Lærdalselva	4.4
Rauma	4.7	Alta	4.3
Surna	4.7	Sandvikselva	4.1
Fosen	4.7	Loneelva	3.9
Gaula	4.6	Luleå	3.1
Etnelva	4.6	Usma	2.3

(2) *Late maturity.* It has already been pointed out that age at sexual maturity in practice sets the upper limit to the size of fish which can be produced in Norwegian salmon and trout farms. Though environmental factors such as temperature and food supply undoubtedy have influence, age at maturity is in part genetically determined and selective breeding for late maturity could increase the maximum size of fish attainable.

(3) *Disease resistance.* There is hope that selective breeding may reduce the problem of vibriosis, the most serious disease commonly encountered on Norwegian marine salmonid farms (Chapter 9). It has already been found that strains of salmon vary greatly in their resistance to this disease (Gjedrem and Aulstad, 1974).

(4) *Carcass quality.* The most desirable traits here are considered to be a body shape which gives maximum meat yield and desirable, *ie* red, flesh colour.

(5) *Conversion efficiency.* Selection for efficient food conversion has been important in breeding farm animals and it is to be expected that genetic differences also occur between strains of salmonids in the efficiency with which they convert their food into meat. Unfortunately it is experimentally quite difficult to measure exactly how much food fish eat, and consequently little routine testing of fish strains for this trait has been done so far. Nevertheless, in other animals there is always a high genetic correlation between growth rate and food conversion, so by selecting for rapid growth in salmonids we may also be selecting for good conversion efficiency.

Before starting a programme of selective breeding for any of these traits it is necessary to know (a) what selection method should be used, and (b) the genetic gain which can be expected.

Selection method

Mass selection, *ie* simply picking the individuals which show the best performance in a particular trait and using them as brood stock, is the only selection method which can be used when the relationships between animals are unknown. However, in salmonids it appears that only one economically important trait can be efficiently selected for by mass selection, namely growth rate. For all other traits family selection, *ie* breeding from the families of fish which show the best performance for the trait, is better. To get information on which to base a programme of family selection it is necessary to test many full and half-sibling groups of fish for their performance in the important traits. (Sibling means having parents in common.) To do this, family groups are at first kept in separate tanks but, once they are large enough, individual fish can be marked by freeze-branding (Refstie and Aulstad, 1975) so that their future performance can be followed in mixed-family populations.

Genetic gain

The expected genetic gain, *ie* the potential for improvement in the performance of fish in a particular trait when selection is applied, can also be calculated. This is important to avoid waste of time and money selecting for traits for which there is little genetic scope for progress, and allow concentration on those likely to give the greatest benefit through selection.

Genetic gain can be calculated from the formula:

$$G = \frac{ih^2 \sigma p}{L} \text{ (Falconer, 1960);}$$

where h^2 is the 'heritability', the ratio of the genetic to the phenotypic

173

variance, and σp is the phenotypic standard deviation. These parameters can be estimated mathematically for any trait from the results of experiments on performance of fish families and individuals. L is the generation interval, which is equivalent to the age of parents at maturity. For rainbow trout this is two or, more usually, three years, and for salmon normally four years where one-year-old smolts are produced. These are similar to generation intervals for farm animals. i is the selection differential, an expression of the intensity with which selection can be applied.

The factors in this equation which lead us to be confident that rapid improvements in salmonids are possible through selection are the phenotypic standard deviation and the selection differential. The higher these figures are, the larger and more rapid are the selection gains to be expected. Because only a small percentage of the individuals in a farmed salmonid population are required for breeding, certainly no more than 1%, a very high selection differential can be applied. The limit imposed on this in practice is the inbreeding depression which can result if too few brood stock are used. The phenotypic variance is expressed as the 'coefficient of variation', and this coefficient tends to be high for important traits in salmonids. As an example, coefficient of variation for growth rate in cattle, sheep and pigs varies from 7% to 17% (Fimland, 1973; Gjedrem, 1967; Standal, 1973). Estimates made for salmonids range between 30% and 70% (Gjedrem, 1975a).

Prospects for improvements through selective breeding are enhanced in Norway by the fact that smolt and fingerling production tends to be concentrated in relatively few, specialist farms. The majority of farmers, who buy these small fish and grow them on to harvest size, are already aware of differences in the quality of the smolts and fingerlings they purchase and are prepared to pay more for 'better' fish. At present better usually means only bigger, but in future we can expect to see higher prices also paid for fish selected for desirable traits other than growth rate. These might be accompanied by documentation as to their genetic background.

Alternative species and hybrids

New species

There seems little prospect in Norway for commercial, controlled culture of fish species other than salmonids in the near future. However, experimental work has been done on the potential of salmonid species other than Atlantic salmon and rainbow trout. The results of tests on sea trout, pink salmon, and migratory races of Arctic char are summarized in *Table* 11, together with comparable data for Atlantic salmon and rainbow trout.

Table 11. Growth of salmonids at the Fish Breeding Experimental Stations at Sunndalsøra and Averøy.

Species	Mean weight at 190 days old (g)	Weight at transfer to sea (g)	Maximum time in sea (months)	Weight at slaughter (kg)
Atlantic salmon	7	25–60	27	4–7
Rainbow trout	53	35–100	13–19	1–5
Sea trout	8	25–75	27	1–2
Arctic char	18	25–75	–	–
Pink salmon	35	2–50	10	0.5–1.0

Growth rates of pink salmon are particularly promising, saleable fish of 0.5–1kg being produced in only one year from the egg. The first commercially produced pink salmon are being sold on the Norwegian market in 1977. They are of course a new and different product for Norway, being much smaller at harvest than the other salmonid species, and it remains to be seen how the market will receive them. However, if they are able to command a price somewhere between that of rainbow trout and Atlantic salmon the prospects for growth of a 'pan-size' pink salmon industry look good.

Preliminary results with Arctic char and sea trout are not so promising. Problems are experienced in keeping char alive all year in sea water. When the time comes for their natural annual migration into fresh water, many of the fish die if kept confined in sea pens (Gjedrem, 1975b). The growth rate of sea trout in floating cages appears to be low compared with Atlantic salmon.

Hybrids

Many interspecific crosses have been made, and survival and growth of the offspring compared with the parent species. All the offspring of crosses where rainbow trout is one parent usually die, but survival of other crosses is often good. Growth of most hybrids is inferior or

Table 12. Average body weight (g) of salmonids and salmonid crosses at 11 months of age (from Refstie and Gjedrem, 1975).

Sperm	Egg			
	Arctic char	Brown trout	Sea trout	Salmon
Arctic char	55.2	58.2	Died	96.5
Brown trout	73.3	41.8	Died	7.7
Sea trout	58.3	24.9	31.8	6.1
Salmon	70.7	7.3	8.8	30.0

intermediate to the parent species (*Table* 12), but where one parent is Arctic char hybrids frequently grow better than either parent species. The cross Arctic char x Atlantic salmon shows particular promise. It is not yet known whether such hybrids will be fertile, but if they are not it may be possible to grow them much larger before harvest than the parent species.

Food studies

Many aspects of the dietary needs of salmon and trout are poorly known, so food manufacturers have to add such things as vitamins in amounts greater than the fish really need, just to make sure the diet is not deficient. As understanding of the fishes' precise food requirements improves through continuing research these wasteful practices will be reduced with consequent economies in food costs. Similarly, better knowledge of the amount and qualities of the basic dietary constituents, *ie* carbohydrates, proteins and fats, required will eventually enable 'least cost' diets to be formulated with the aid of computers according to the availability and market price of food components. In particular the use of cheaper sources of protein to replace part of the expensive fishmeal portion of diets can be expected to increase.

Ocean ranching

As an alternative to growing-on salmon in floating net cages, as currently practised in Norway, smolts can be released to run out to sea and harvested in traps or nets on their return towards the rivers to spawn as adults. This approach is already proving highly successful with the Pacific chum salmon (*Oncorhynchus keta*) in northern Japan, and there is much interest in it in the USA. There are ocean ranching industries based on Atlantic salmon in Iceland and Sweden.

Basically, the advantage of ocean ranching over cage culture is that the salmon do not have to be artificially fed during their rapid-growing sea water lives. This not only means a huge saving in production costs but also a more 'biologically rational' operation, because when we harvest the salmon on their return to the rivers we are taking 'new' protein which the fish have accumulated in their bodies while feeding themselves in the sea. In cage culture salmon have to be fed largely on other species of fish already caught from the sea by the commercial fishing fleet.

The greatest disadvantage of ocean ranching is that survival of salmon during their free life in the sea is often poor, and only a small proportion of the fish released as smolts return to the rivers as adults. Whether or not ocean ranching is economically viable, therefore, depends on the ratio of

176

the sale value of returning adults to the cost of smolt production and adult capture.

The percentage of salmon returning varies greatly from place to place. In Norway, returns of Atlantic salmon are usually low, around 1 or 2% at most. It would be economically worthwhile to release Pacific salmon, with their short fresh water life, for this sort of return, but for Atlantic salmon requiring over a year to smoltification it is not. Even at a reliable 2% return, a simple calculation shows that each adult salmon returning would cost almost NKr 300 for smolts alone (at Kr 5.75 per smolt, Chapter 10), above the market value of an average-sized spawner of 4 or 5 kg. The costs of capture must be added to this. At present in Norway, therefore, it is better to keep the smolts and grow them on in cages, where survival is often over 80%, rather than releasing them, the vast majority never to be seen again.

However, work is being done to find ways in which percentage returns could be increased. Indications have been obtained that returns of salmon are higher if larger smolts are released. Also, in Sweden Carlin (1969) has found that some strains of salmon consistently show larger percentage returns than others (*Fig* 78). Use of the best strains, and future selective breeding from these, may increase returns to economic levels in the foreseeable future.

Sea trout may have advantages for ocean ranching as they do not move as far out into the sea as salmon, often staying in the area of the fjord into which they were released. Fishing pressure on them can therefore be controlled during their whole life cycle by Norway alone, unlike salmon which are vulnerable to fishing as a result of foreign government decisions.

Early maturation

Until very recently early sexual maturation has been no problem on Norwegian salmon farms. For most farms this is still the case, and salmon can safely be left for a full two years in the sea, with under 5% maturing after one year. However, one or two of the largest companies in the country are now reporting that up to 30% or even 40% of their fish are maturing after only one year in the sea, with subsequent disastrously reduced growth in the second year. This problem as yet affects only a small percentage of fish farmed in Norway, but it has also been a major problem to many producers in Scotland, and the possibility that it might increase in Norway in future must be recognized.

No-one is sure what causes early maturation, but some people think it might be the result of the higher food quality and quantity received by the

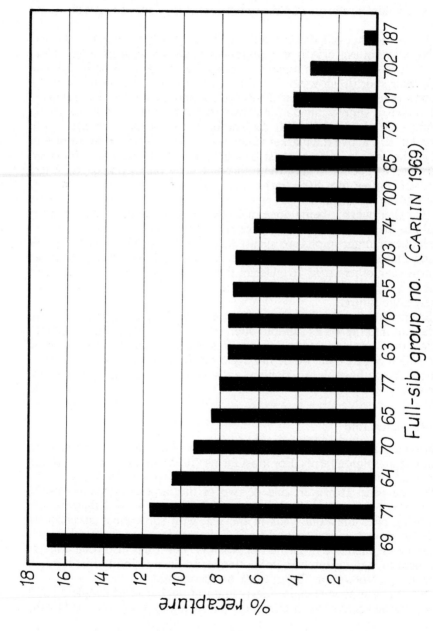

Fig 78. Percentage returns of different salmon strains. *(From Carlin, 1969).*

fish in farms than under natural conditions in the wild. To date it has been usual to feed fish, if possible, as much as they will eat during their entire sea water life, in order to obtain maximal growth. However, it has recently been suggested that feeding should be limited for the first six months in the sea, *ie* up until the first winter, in an attempt to stop the fish maturing early. It must be stressed that there is no evidence that this would work, or even that heavy feeding is mainly responsible for early maturation, but experiments will certainly be done to test this hypothesis in the near future.

Alternative approaches through selective breeding for late maturity and the development of species crosses which may be sterile are discussed above. It is possible to produce sterile fish by adding sex hormones to the diet, but these may leave residues in the meat and make this technique unacceptable in fish for human consumption.

Triploid fish, *ie* fish possessing three sets of chromosomes instead of the usual two (diploid), are normally sterile. In plaice it is possible to produce triploid fish by subjecting newly fertilized eggs to cold shocks (Purdom, 1972). The effect of this is to double the number of maternal chromosomes, which together with the chromosomes of the sperm produce fish with three sets of chromosomes. This technique has been attempted with salmon (Lincoln *et al.*, 1974), but has so far been unsuccessful. More promising results have been obtained by using cytochalasin B on fertilized eggs of salmon and rainbow trout (Refstie *et al.*, 1977). In some eggs this drug doubles the number of chromosomes and, if the resulting tetraploid fish survive to maturity, their gametes should be diploid (instead of the normal haploid) and form triploid offspring when crossed with normal fish. Such possible solutions to early maturation are so far only in the early stages of experimentation. However, the research effort given to this problem is being increased in the hope that solutions can be found before national production of salmon is significantly affected.

TEACHING AND ADVISORY SERVICES

Terrestrial farmers can get advice on latest techniques from their local Farm Advisory Officer. There is no equivalent service to advise fish farmers and it would be very expensive to provide trained people specially for this purpose. Advice can currently be obtained from the appropriate government departments listed in the Appendix, but nevertheless there is a need for more individual advice to be available at a local level. Most Farm Advisory Officers are trained at the Agricultural University of

179

Norway, and the course in salmonid culture now offered by the Department of Animal Genetics and Breeding at this University should go some way towards enabling Farm Advisory Service personnel to fill this need. A course in aquaculture is also offered by the Institute of Fisheries Research at the University of Tromsø.

An annual short course for practising fish farmers, designed to bring them up-to-date with latest techniques, is run by the Institute of Marine Research at Bergen. Starting in 1977, a similar course is being given by the Agricultural University of Norway in collaboration with the Norwegian Agricultural Research Council and the County authorities of Møre and Romsdal, an area in the heart of Norway's 'fish farming belt'. These organizations, partly funded by a grant from the American Kellogg Foundation, will also offer year-long specialist courses to Agricultural School students, and shorter courses to younger, High School students. It is hoped that these courses will provide a nucleus of teachers, advisors and informed practising fish farmers who will help ensure that the future development of salmonid farming in Norway is not hindered by lack of skilled personnel.

Appendix

List of organizations and institutions with administrative or technical responsibilities involving salmon or trout farming in Norway. (This list does not include every organization in any way connected with Norwegian salmonid farming, but it is sufficient to enable the reader to obtain further information on any aspect of the industry by writing to the appropriate address listed).

1. Norwegian Fish Farmers' Association

c/o Det Kgl. Selskap for Norges Vel, Rosenkrantzgate 8, Oslo 1. (Secretary Mr Lars Bull-Berg).

The main 'trade union' for Norwegian fish farmers, representing their interests to government and industry. Also helps set prices for fish and does sales promotion work.

2. Directorate of Fisheries.

(*a*) *Head Office*. Møllendalsveien 4, Postbox 185, N–5001 Bergen. (Director of fisheries Mr Knut Vartdal).

Fisheries administration, including licencing and inspection of fish farms.

(*b*) *Institute of Marine Research*. Nordnesparken 2, Postbox 2906, 5011 Bergen-Nordnes. (Research leader Dr Dag Møller).

Research on all aspects of marine fisheries, including sea culture of salmonids in floating cages.

(*c*) *Government Vitamin Institute*. Lars Hilles gate 26, Postbox 187, N–5001 Bergen. (Professor Dr Olaf Braekken).

Research on nutrition relevant to the development of improved diets for salmonid culture.

(*d*) *Department of Quality Control*. Postbox 185, 5001 Bergen. (Chief inspector Mr S Skilbrei).

Has a team of inspectors at ports to ensure good quality of fish, including farmed salmonids.

(*e*) *Department of Fishery Economics*. Postbox 185, 5001 Bergen. (Director Mr Per Mietle).

Gathers statistics on fish production, including farmed salmonids.

(*f*) *Fish and Research*. 5198 Matredal. (Officer-in-charge Mr Oscar Ingebrigtsen).

Research on culture of salmonids from the egg to maturity including growth, feeding, disease, breeding and environmental studies.

181

3. Directorate of Wildlife and Freshwater Fish

(a) *Office for Fresh Water Fish.* Elgesetergate 10, 7000 Trondheim. (There are also five other district offices in various parts of the country).

Responsible for enforcing regulations covering fresh water fisheries including angling, commercial netting, and capture of brood stock for fish farms. Also re-stock waters with young fish.

(d) *Fish Research Division.* Postbox 63, 1432 Aas-NLH. (Research leader Dr L Rosseland).

Research primarily on wild populations of fresh water fish, especially salmonids.

(c) *Ims Research Station.* 4300 Sandnes. (Officer-in-charge Dr C Senstad).

Research primarily on wild salmonids, but a smolt production unit is under construction.

4. Department of Animal Genetics and Breeding, Agricultural University of Norway

(a) *Head Office.* Postbox 24, 1432 Aas-NLH. (Professor Dr Harald Skjervold, Research leader (fish) Dr Trygve Gjedrem).

Research on many aspects of salmonid culture, especially selective breeding and other genetic work. Also runs a teaching course in salmonid culture.

(b) *Fish Breeding Experimental Station.* 6600 Sunndalsøra. (Manager Mr Arne Kittelsen).

Research as 4a, also commercial production of smolts and fingerlings.

(c) *Fish Breeding Experimental Station.* 6553 Ekkilsøy. (Manager Mr Johann Saettem).

Research as 4a, also commercial production of large salmon and rainbow trout in floating cages.

(d) *Breeding Station for Brown Trout.* 3577 Hovet. (Manager Mr Hallvard Søndrål).
Production of brown trout for re-stocking natural waters and research on their selective breeding.

(e) *Marnardal Trout Hatchery.* 4534 Marnardal. (Manager Mrs Aslaug Ågedal).
Research on selective breeding of salmonids to produce strains tolerant to low pH.

5. Department of Poultry and Fur-Animal Science, Agricultural University of Norway

Postbox 17, 1432 Aas-NLH. (Professor Dr Harald Hvidsten).
Research on nutrition leading to formulation of better diets for salmonid culture.

6. Chr. Michelsens Institute

Nygårdsgate 114, 5000 Bergen. (Research leader Dr Ole Devik).
Research on technical and engineering aspects of salmonid farming including design of net cages, detailed planning of unit construction, and site selection.

7. Institute of Fishery Economics

5000 Bergen. (Professor G M Gerhardsen).
Gathers statistics on economics of fish farming operations and gives advice on the basis of these.

8. Department of Zoology, University of Oslo
Blindern, Oslo 3.
Research on salmonids relevant to culture and exploitation of wild populations, including homing of salmon.

9. Institute of Fisheries Research, University of Tromsø
Postbox 790, 9001 Tromsø.
Research on culture of salmonids in floating cages.

10. Norwegian Meat Marketing Board
Lørenveien 37, Oslo.
Cooperative organization for production and sales of farmed fish.

11. Norwegian Export Committee for Fresh Fish
Parkgate 6, 6000 Ålesund. (Director Mr J Muri).
Licences for shipping fish, and collation of fishery statistics.

12. Norwegian Trout Sales Organization
Parkgate 6, 6000 Ålesund.
Second representative body for Norwegian trout farmers. Organizes selling of trout within Norway.

13. Norwegian District Development Fund
Møllergate 1–3, Oslo 1.
Guarantees loans for setting up fish farms.

14. Norwegian Export Council
Drammensveien 40, Oslo 2.
Has representatives all over the world to promote exports of Norwegian goods, including farmed salmonids.

15. Norwegian Institute of Food Research
Postbox 50, 1432 Aas-NLH.
Research on quality of flesh in farmed salmonids.

16. Veterinary Department
C J Hambros pl. 5, Oslo. (Veterinary inspector Olav Gladhaug).
Legal responsibility for inspection of fish farms for disease.

17. Norwegian Veterinary Institute
Ullevälsveien 68, Oslo. (Veterinary inspector Dr Tore Håstein).
Research on fish disease diagnosis and control. Co-operation in fish farm inspection and certification with 16.

18. Norwegian Veterinary College
Postbox 8156, Oslo-Dep, Oslo 1.
Research on fish diseases, especially drug development.

19. Department of Fisheries
Drammensveien 20, Oslo-Dep, Oslo 1.
Responsible for formulating regulations and for licencing of fish farms.

References

Austreng E (1976a). Fat and protein in diets for salmonid fishes. I. Fat content in dry diets for salmon parr (*Salmo salar* L). *Meld. Norg. LandbrHøgsk.* 55(5): 16pp. (In Norwegian with English summary).

Austreng E (1976b). Fat and protein in diets for salmonid fishes. II. Fat content in dry diets for rainbow trout (*Salmo gairdnerii* Richardson). *Meld. Norg. LandbrHøgsk.* 55(6): 14pp. (In Norwegian with English summary).

Austreng E (1976c). Fat and protein in diets for salmonid fishes. III. Different types of fat in dry diets for rainbow trout (*Salmo gairdnerii* Richardson). *Meld. Norg. LandbrHøgsk.* 55(7): 18pp. (In Norwegian with English summary).

Bergsjø T and Vassvik V (1977). *Gyrodactylus* — en sjelden, men plagsom fiskeparasitt. *Norsk fiskeoppdrett.* 4(2): 11–13. (In Norwegian).

Brandal P O and Egidius E (1977). Preliminary report on oral treatment against salmon lice, *Lepeophtheirus salmonis*, with Neguvon. *Aquaculture 10*: 177–178.

Braaten B R and Sætre R (1973). Oppdrett av laksefisk i Norske kystfarvann. Miljø og anleggstyper. *Fisken og Havet, series B(2)*: 1–88. Fiskeridirektoratets Havforskningsinstitutt, Bergen. (In Norwegian).

Carlin B (1969). Salmon tagging experiments. *Laxforskningsinstitutet Meddelande* 2–4, Sweden.

Donaldson L R and Olson R R (1957). Development of rainbow trout brood stock by selective breeding. *Trans. Am. Fish. Soc.* 85: 93–101.

Falconer D S (1960). *Introduction to quantitative genetics*. The Ronald Press Company, New York. 365pp.

Fimland E (1973). Estimates of phenotypic and genetic parameters for growth characteristics of young potential AI bulls. *Acta Agric. Scand.* 23: 209–216.

Gjedrem T (1967). Phenotypic and genetic parameters for weight of lambs at five ages. *Acta Agric. Scand.* 17: 199–216.

Gjedrem T (1974). Oppdrett av laksefisk. *Lecture notes, Department of Animal Genetics and Breeding, Agricultural University of Norway*. 143pp. (In Norwegian).

Gjedrem T (1975a). Possibilities for genetic gain in salmonids. *Aquaculture 6*: 23–29.

Gjedrem T (1975b). Survival of Arctic char in the sea during fall and winter. *Aquaculture 6*: 189–190.

Gjedrem T (1976a). Genetic variation in tolerance of brown trout to acid water. *SNSF-project*, Norway, FR5/76: 11pp.

Gjedrem T (1976b). Possibilities for genetic improvements in salmonids. *J. Fish. Res. Bd. Can.* 33(4): 1094–1099.

Gjedrem T and Aulstad D (1974). Selection experiments with salmon. I. Differences in resistance to vibrio disease of salmon parr (*Salmo salar*). *Aquaculture 3*: 51–59.

Halver J E (Ed.) (1972). *Fish nutrition*. Academic Press, New York. 713pp.

Hildingstam J (1976). Economics of research and development in the sea farming of salmonid species. *Fish Farming International* 3(1): 16–19.

Hoffman G L and Meyer F P(1974). *Parasites of fresh water fishes*. TFH Publications, Neptune City, New Jersey. 224pp.

Liao P B (1971). Water requirements of salmonids. *Progve. Fish-Cult.* 33(4): 210–215.

Lincoln R F, Aulstad D and Grammeltvedt A (1974). Attempted triploid induction in Atlantic salmon (*Salmo salar*) using cold shocks. *Aquaculture 4*: 287–297.

McCay C M and Tunison A V (1935). *Rept. Exp. Work Cortland Hatchery Year 1934*. NY Conservation Department, Albany, New York.

Milne P H (1972). *Fish and shellfish farming in coastal waters*. Fishing News Books Ltd., Farnham, Surrey, England. 208pp.

Phillips A M and Brockway P R (1959). Dietary calories and the production of trout in hatcheries. *Progve. Fish-Cult 21*: 3–16.

Phillips A M, Tunison A S and Brockway D R (1948). The utilization of carbohydrates by trout. *Fish. Res. Bull.* NY. 11: 5–44.

Purdom C E (1972). Induced polyploidy in plaice (*Pleuronectes platessa*) and its hybrid with the flounder (*Platichthys flesus*). *Heredity*, London, 29(1): 11–24.

Refstie T (1977). Effect of density on growth and survival of rainbow trout. *Aquaculture*. 11(4): 329–334.

Refstie T and Aulstad D (1975). Tagging experiments with salmonids. *Aquaculture 5*: 367–374.

Refstie T and Gjedrem T (1975). Hybrids between salmonidae species. Hatchability and growth rate in the freshwater period. *Aquaculture 6*: 333–342.

Refstie T and Kittelsen A (1976). Effect of density on growth and survival of artificially reared Atlantic salmon. *Aquaculture 8*: 319–326.

Refstie T, Vassvik V and Gjedrem T (1977). Induction of polyploidy in salmonids by cytochalasin B. *Aquaculture 10*: 65–74.

Risa S and Skjervold H (1975). Water re-use system for smolt production. *Aquaculture 6*: 191–195.

Roberts R J and Shepherd C J (1974). *Handbook of trout and salmon diseases*. Fishing News Books Ltd., Farnham, Surrey, England. 168pp.

Senstad C (1975). Lokalisering og utforming av settefiskanlegg. In: *Fiskeoppdrett*, Landbruksforlaget, Oslo, 117–130. (In Norwegian).

Skjervold H (1973). *Vannbehov ved oppdrett av ørret og laks*. Department of Animal Genetics and Breeding, Agricultural University of Norway. Mimeograph. (In Norwegian).

Skjervold H (1975). Oppdrett av laks og ørret — et alternativ i samband med distriktsutbyggingen. In: *Fiskeoppdrett*, Landbruksforlaget, Oslo, 17–29. (In Norwegian).

Standal N (1973). Studies on breeding and selection schemes in pigs. III. The effect of parity and litter size on the 'on-the-farm' testing results. *Acta. Agric. Scand.* 23: 225–231.

Tunison A V, Brockway D R, Maxwell J M, Dorr A L and McCay C M (1942). *Cortland hatchery report No. 11,* NY Conservation Department, Albany, New York.

INDEX

Acclimatization, 8, 37, 48, 57–59, 78
Acid precipitation, 29
Acidity—see Water, pH
Agricultural Development Fund, 7
Agricultural University of Norway, 179–180
Alevins—see Fry
Anadromous species, 8
Anaesthetics, 38, 61, 143
Angling, 11
Antibiotics, 137, 139
Appetite, 21, 110, 122, 123, 137
Arctic char—see Char
Astaxanthin, 130–131
Astra-Ewos A/B, 40, 48, 115, 124, 125
Atlantic salmon—see Salmon

Baltic current, 3–4
Binding meals, 107, 109–110, 112, 131
Biological filters, 23–24
Bjordal, 79
Blood meal, 119
Bleeding, 142–143
Boats, live-hauling, 37, 62–64, 84, 99, 142
Breeding goals, 171–173

Brood stock, 18, 36–39, 97, 107, 171–174

Cage culture—see Net cages
Cannibalism, 49
Canthaxanthin, 131
Carbohydrate, 105–106, 110, 119, 176
Carotenoids, 130–131
Capelin, 107–108, 119, 131
Char, Arctic, 8–11, 37, 43, 137, 174–176
Chilodonella, 135
Chlorobutanol, 38
Coalfish, 63, 84, 108
Cod, 63, 84, 108, 119
Commercial fishing, 1–2, 11, 18, 63, 84, 108, 140, 142, 166, 168, 169, 176, 177
Compressed air, 16, 123, 124, 126–127, 129–130
Compressors, 16, 31, 61, 123, 126–127, 129
Conversion efficiency, 132, 133, 173
Copper, 25, 94
Costia, 134–135
Currents, 2–4, 67–68, 71, 76, 79, 83, 98, 102
Cytochalasin B, 179

188

Infectious pancreatic necrosis (IPN), 138
Inka de-gassing apparatus, 26–28
Institute of Fisheries Research, University of Tromsø, 180
Institute of Marine Research, 83, 180
Iron, 31

Japan, 176

Kellogg Foundation, 180
Kelts, 9
Kidney disease, 138

Lepeophtheirus—see Sea lice
Licencing, 69, 139
Life cycles,
    Fish, 8–10
    Parasites, 134–137
Live-hauling boats—see Boats

Mackerel, 119
Malachite green, 44, 136, 139
Marketing, 140–151
Markets, 147–148
Maturation—see Sexual maturity
Metals, 31
Milt—see Sperm
Minerals, 107, 110, 112, 119
Ministry of Agriculture, 139
Ministry of Health, 139
Mortality, 17, 18, 26, 37, 44, 47–48, 49, 59, 74, 100, 106, 155, 163, 166, 169, 170, 176–177
Mowi A/S, 6, 62, 70–77, 83, 103, 109, 112–114, 129, 131, 145, 166
MS 222, 38

Neguvon, 138
Net cages, 6, 7, 18, 19, 61, 62, 64, 65, 67, 68, 76–77, 79, 81, 83, 84–104, 110, 111, 123, 124, 127, 128, 129, 130, 133, 138, 142, 153, 154, 156, 157, 158, 161, 162, 165, 175, 176
    Floating framework, 84, 85–91
    Moorings, 91, 94–97, 154
    Net bags, 84–85, 86, 91–94
Netting enclosures—see Enclosures
Nitrogen supersaturation—see Supersaturation
Norsildmel (Norwegian herring oil and herring meal sales organization), 119
Norsk Hydro A/S, 167
Norwegian Agricultural Research Council, 180
Norwegian Fish Farmers' Association, 6, 149, 151–152
Norwegian Meat Marketing Board, 151
Norwegian Trout Sales Organization, 150–151
Norwegian Veterinary Institute, 139

Ocean ranching, 176–177
Oily fish, 107–108
Osland, Mr. Erling, 81–83
Ova—see Eggs
Ownership of land, 34, 68–69
Oxygen, 3, 23, 26, 29, 31, 32, 34, 46, 49, 56, 57, 61, 64, 66–67, 74, 76, 83, 92, 96, 98, 100–101, 131, 136
Oxygenation, 16, 23, 72, 74, 101
Oxytetracycline, 137, 139

Sea, 8, 10, 11, 174–175, 177
Steelhead, 57

Ulcerative dermal necrosis (UDN), 138
Ulcer disease, 138
United Kingdom, 29, 166
USA, 26, 42, 53, 107, 116, 138, 147, 176

Vaccination, 138
Vacuum fish pumps—see Pumps
Veløykjølpo, 70–72, 74–76, 112
Vibrio, 137–138, 172
Vik brothers, 3, 85
Viral haemorrhagic septicemia (VHS), 138
Viruses, 36, 138
Vitamins, 107, 110, 112, 115, 116, 120, 176

Water, fresh,
pH, 23, 27, 29

Quality, 21, 27–31, 56–57, 65, 134
Quantity, 21, 32–34, 43, 49, 53
Sources, 31–32
Temperature—see Temperature
Water, sea,
Quality, 58, 66–67
Wet foods—see Food
Whirling disease, 52–53, 138
White fish, 107, 108
White spot disease—see *Ichthyophthirius*
Wholesalers, 142, 147, 149, 151

Yolk sac, 9, 46–48

Zinc, 31, 136

Øksna-Bruk A/S, 15–16, 18, 20, 129
Øyerhamn, 62, 129

Other books published by
Fishing News Books Limited
Farnham, Surrey, England

Free catalogue available on request
A living from lobsters
Advances in aquaculture
Aquaculture practices in Taiwan
Better angling with simple science
British freshwater fishes
Coastal aquaculture in the Indo-Pacific region
Commercial fishing methods
Control of fish quality
Culture of bivalve molluscs
Eel capture, culture, processing and marketing
Eel culture
European inland water fish: a multilingual catalogue
FAO catalogue of fishing gear designs
FAO catalogue of small scale fishing gear
FAO investigates ferro-cement fishing craft
Farming the edge of the sea
Fish and shellfish farming in coastal waters
Fish catching methods of the world
Fish farming international No 2
Fish inspection and quality control
Fisheries oceanography
Fishery products
Fishing boats of the world 1
Fishing boats of the world 2
Fishing boats of the world 3
Fishing ports and markets
Fishing with electricity
Fishing with light

Freezing and irradiation of fish
Handbook of trout and salmon diseases
Handy medical guide for seafarers
How to make and set nets
Inshore fishing: its skills, risks, rewards
International regulation of marine fisheries: a study of regional fisheries organizations
Marine pollution and sea life
Mechanization of small fishing craft
Mending of fishing nets
Modern deep sea trawling gear
Modern fishing gear of the world 1
Modern fishing gear of the world 2
Modern fishing gear of the world 3
Modern inshore fishing gear
More Scottish fishing craft and their work
Multilingual dictionary of fish and fish products
Navigation primer for fishermen
Netting materials for fishing gear
Pair trawling and pair seining—the technology of two boat fishing
Pelagic and semi-pelagic trawling gear
Planning of aquaculture development—an introductory guide
Power transmission and automation for ships and submersibles
Refrigeration on fishing vessels
Salmon fisheries of Scotland
Seafood fishing for amateur and professional
Ships' gear 66
Sonar in fisheries: a forward look
Stability and trim of fishing vessels
Testing the freshness of frozen fish
Textbook of fish culture; breeding and cultivation of fish
The fertile sea
The fish resources of the ocean
The fishing cadet's handbook
The lemon sole
The marketing of shellfish
The seine net: its origin, evolution and use
The stern trawler
The stocks of whales
Trawlermen's handbook
Tuna: distribution and migration
Underwater observation using sonar